SCIENCE ENCYCLOPEDIAS

THE WEATHER ENCYCLOPEDIA

BY JANINE UNGVARSKY

Abdo Reference

An Imprint of Abdo Publishing
abdobooks.com

TABLE OF CONTENTS

WEATHER BASICS 4
   What Is Weather?.. 4
   Weather Is in the Atmosphere............ 10
   Weather and the Sun 12
   Weather and the Air 14
   The Climate Is Changing 24
   Natural Causes of a
      Changing Climate................................. 28
   Human Causes of Climate Change 34
   Weather Phenomena............................. 40
   Clouds 42
   Precipitation.. 52
   Basic Types of Precipitation 54
   Dew, Frost, and Fog 64
   Other Weather Phenomena 68
   Clear-Sky Phenomena 76
   Light Phenomena 80
   Weather Forecasting.............................. 86

EXTREME STORMS 94
   What Is Extreme Weather?................... 94
   Thunderstorms 104
   Floods... 110
   Hurricanes... 116
   Tornadoes 126
   Hailstorms 134
   Blizzards... 138
   Ice Storms 146
   Droughts 150
   Wildfires and Firestorms 156
   Dust Storms... 160
   Heat Waves 164
   Special Storm Types 170
   Other Extreme Weather Events......... 178

**HOW CLIMATE CHANGE
IMPACTS EXTREME STORMS............. 184**

GLOSSARY 188

TO LEARN MORE................................ 189

INDEX 190

PHOTO CREDITS 191

WEATHER BASICS:
WHAT IS WEATHER?

The natural events that happen in the air surrounding Earth are called weather. Weather can be calm and comfortable. It can produce a sunny day with a warm breeze. It can also be dangerous, creating blizzards, tornadoes, and hurricanes.

Each part of Earth has weather conditions that change on a daily basis. Each part also has a pattern of weather that can be seen over a long period of time. For example, some areas get

To many people, a warm, sunny day is an example of ideal weather.

A lack of rain in an area's climate affects that region's plants, animals, and landscapes.

a lot of rain while others get very little. Some areas stay warm or cold all year. Others have wide changes in temperature at different times of the year. Patterns of weather over years, decades, and even centuries are called the area's climate.

Both weather and climate affect people, animals, plants, and the landscape. People wear different clothing based on how warm or cold the weather is. Some plants and animals cannot live in places that stay very hot or cold. Temperature changes can affect water in the ground. Hot conditions can dry out the

WEATHER BASICS: WHAT IS WEATHER?

ground, making the land dusty. Cold conditions can freeze water into ice, cracking natural rocks or paved streets.

Weather also affects the kinds of homes people live in. In cold areas, homes need heating and insulation. Homes in hot climates might not have heaters at all. Instead, they are designed to keep cool. The structures and materials may allow less sunlight to get inside. People also build their homes to withstand extreme weather. In areas where there are a lot of floods, houses are often built on stilts to protect them. Homes in areas that get a

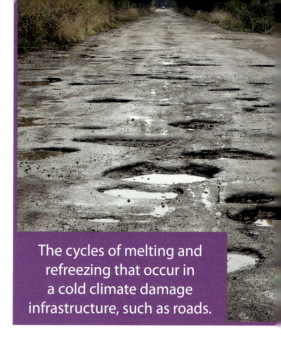

The cycles of melting and refreezing that occur in a cold climate damage infrastructure, such as roads.

In some regions, weather can become so severe that people build shelters to protect themselves from it.

lot of hurricanes and tornadoes are sturdy to stand up to strong winds, and they may have basements for shelter.

The food people eat is also affected by weather and climate. Many crops need a certain temperature and amount of rain to grow well. Droughts, which are long periods without rain, and cold spells can kill crops and animals used for food. Before people had ways to safely transport and store food in

Drought conditions bring widespread devastation to critical food sources.

WEATHER BASICS: WHAT IS WEATHER?

different weather, bad weather often caused big problems. It meant people either moved to a new area with better weather or faced starvation. This still happens in areas of the world that lack access to safe food transportation.

People often choose to live in an area because of its climate. Some people like living where it is warm all the time. Others

Mild weather may make it easier to raise animals and grow crops for a living.

prefer to have seasons that change throughout the year. Farmers and ranchers choose areas where the climate is right for their crops or animals. People also avoid living in some areas because of the climate. For example, people might choose not to live in areas that get a lot of snow. They may avoid moving to regions that get a lot of tornadoes, hurricanes, or droughts.

WEATHER IS IN THE ATMOSPHERE

The air around Earth is called the atmosphere. It is densest near the ground. It becomes thinner at high altitudes. From the ground upward, the atmosphere has five layers: the troposphere, stratosphere, mesosphere, thermosphere, and exosphere.

There is no clear boundary between the atmosphere and outer space. One common dividing point is an altitude of 62 miles (100 km). Above this, there are still air molecules. But the air is too thin for an airplane's wings to generate lift. The troposphere includes the air that makes life possible on Earth. It is also where weather happens.

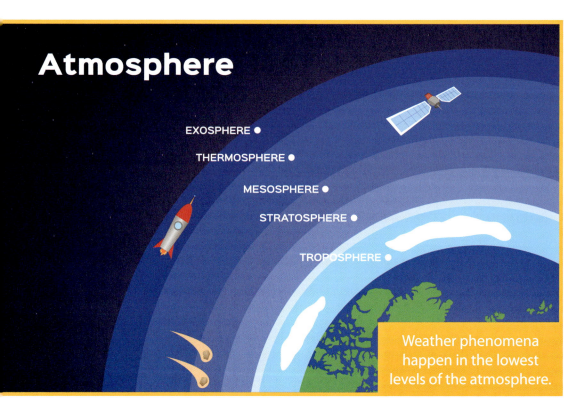

Weather phenomena happen in the lowest levels of the atmosphere.

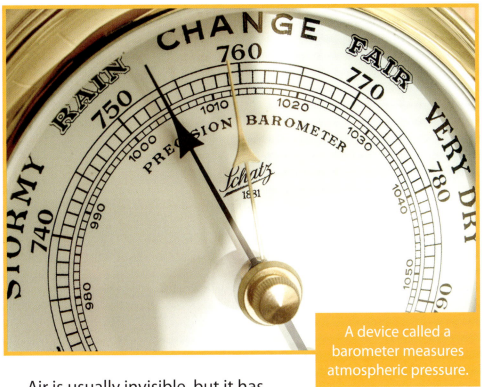

A device called a barometer measures atmospheric pressure.

Air is usually invisible, but it has weight. At sea level, a 1-inch (2.54 cm) square on the ground has about 15 pounds (6.8 kg) of air pushing down on it. In other words, that 1-inch column of air stretching from the ground to space weighs about 15 pounds (6.8 kg). The force of the air pressing on the things around it is known as atmospheric pressure.

Atmospheric pressure does not stay the same all the time. It is affected by heat and moisture. When these things change the atmospheric pressure, Earth's weather also changes. One of the biggest factors in these weather changes is the sun.

WEATHER AND THE SUN

Energy from the sun drives Earth's weather.

Even though the sun is about 93 million miles (150 million km) away, it has a big effect on Earth's weather. The rays of light coming from the sun are called solar energy. Some of this energy reflects off Earth's atmosphere and bounces back out into space. Some of the energy gets through the atmosphere to warm the air and ground.

The amount of solar energy that reaches a place on Earth depends on the angle of sunlight hitting that place. Earth's tilt means that sunlight hits areas near the equator more directly. These regions tend to be hotter. Places closer to the poles receive sunlight at an angle. They tend to be colder. How close the sun is to Earth is not as important. In fact, when the northern hemisphere experiences winter, Earth is closest to the sun. But the northern hemisphere does not receive sunlight at a direct angle at this time, making the regions there colder.

Earth's tilt causes the seasons that different parts of the planet experience.

WEATHER AND THE AIR

Temperature changes affect the air in the atmosphere. The air in the atmosphere is made up of different gases. Nitrogen is the most abundant, making up 78 percent of the atmosphere. Next is oxygen, the gas that people and animals breathe, at 21 percent. The remaining 1 percent is a variety of other gases.

Heat makes the atmosphere's air expand, or fill a bigger space, like a balloon being blown up. When there is less energy from the sun, the air cools. This makes it contract, like a balloon losing its air. When gases expand, they become less dense and move higher up in the atmosphere. A common example of this is the way steam rises up from a hot pot. On the other hand, cold air sinks. It is denser than warm air. It stays closer to the ground. When the sun's energy warms the ground, the heat of the ground warms the air and makes it rise. Then cooler air moves in again to replace the rising warm air. This movement of warmer and cooler air is called convection.

Just as steam rises from a boiling pot of water, warm air rises in the atmosphere.

The convection process is affected by a number of things on Earth. The temperatures of oceans and other large bodies of water are usually warmer or cooler than the land nearby. Sandy deserts are hot and dry. Mountains and other higher areas of land can block and change the flow of air. In cities, structures such as roads, pavement, and buildings absorb more heat than the landscapes they replaced.

All of these things affect air temperature. They create pockets of warmer and cooler air that move around and bump into each other. Meteorologists, the scientists who study weather, call these air pockets high- and low-pressure systems. The gases in a low-pressure system are more spread out, so they rise. High-pressure systems

The vast amount of pavement in large cities absorbs the sun's heat, keeping these areas warmer than they would be otherwise.

WEATHER AND THE AIR

are denser, so they are heavier and sink. When the heat from a warm area on Earth warms the air and makes it rise, it creates an area of low pressure. Cooler air rushes in to replace the warm air in the convection process. This creates a new area of high pressure.

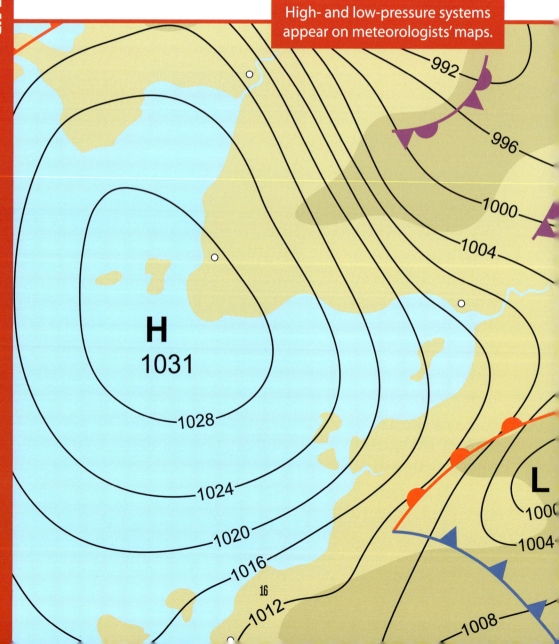

High- and low-pressure systems appear on meteorologists' maps.

A NASA satellite captured a picture of a low-pressure system spinning counterclockwise near Iceland.

In the Northern Hemisphere, the air currents in a low-pressure system spin counterclockwise. High-pressure system air currents spin clockwise. In the Southern Hemisphere, the directions are reversed due to the rotation of the planet. When these systems spin in a full circle around a center point, meteorologists give them a special name. Low-pressure systems are called cyclones and high-pressure systems are called anti-cyclones. Low-pressure systems that reach cyclone status often cause storms.

Air naturally moves from high-pressure areas into low-pressure areas. This phenomenon is known as diffusion. The movements of high- and low-pressure areas through this process make air currents. When warmer and cooler air currents move past each other, they create wind. When there is only a minor difference in temperature between the air currents, they

WEATHER AND THE AIR

diffuse slowly. This makes a gentle breeze. When there is a big difference, the wind blows more strongly. Meteorologists call the place where two air currents come together a front.

There are four main kinds of fronts: warm fronts, cold fronts, stationary fronts, and occluded fronts. Warm fronts happen when warmer air moves into colder air. Cold fronts happen when colder air moves into warmer air. Stationary fronts happen when masses of warm air and masses of cold air push

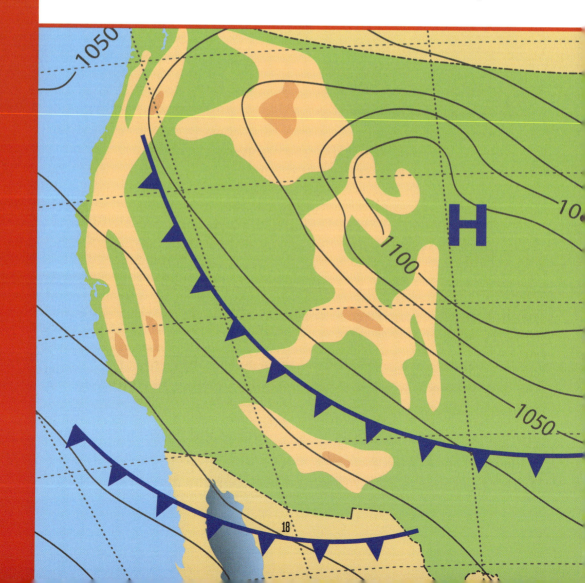

against each other but neither one is strong enough to move the other. Sometimes when warm air moves into cold air, more cold air is following right behind it. Cold air currents move faster than warm air currents, so the second mass of cold air passes the warm air, pushes it out of the way, and moves into the first cold air mass. This creates what meteorologists call an occluded front.

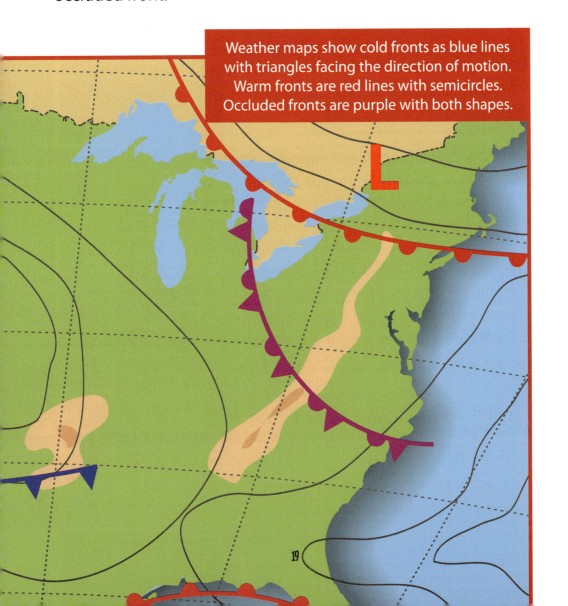

Weather maps show cold fronts as blue lines with triangles facing the direction of motion. Warm fronts are red lines with semicircles. Occluded fronts are purple with both shapes.

WEATHER AND THE AIR

Occluded fronts are sometimes linked with stormy weather.

Occluded fronts can be divided into cold and warm occlusions. In a cold occlusion, the cold air that passes the warm air is colder than the cool air ahead. The temperature drops after a cold occlusion goes through. In a warm occlusion, the cold air that passes the warm air is warmer than the cool air ahead. The temperature rises after a warm occlusion.

The movement of air currents and fronts is also affected by jet streams. Jet streams are thin bands of very strong winds. They are found in the upper troposphere, about 6 miles (9.7 km) above the ground. Jet streams form at the boundary areas between hot and cold air masses. They usually move from the west toward the east.

Several things affect the location and strength of jet streams. They happen most often in winter, because that is

Jet streams are found above most weather phenomena, around the altitude where airliners fly.

when the boundaries between hot and cold air masses are the most intense. The sun can also affect a jet stream. When the sun provides more direct light in spring and summer, the jet stream moves toward one of Earth's poles. Meteorologists call this a ridge. When the fall and winter approach, the sun is at a

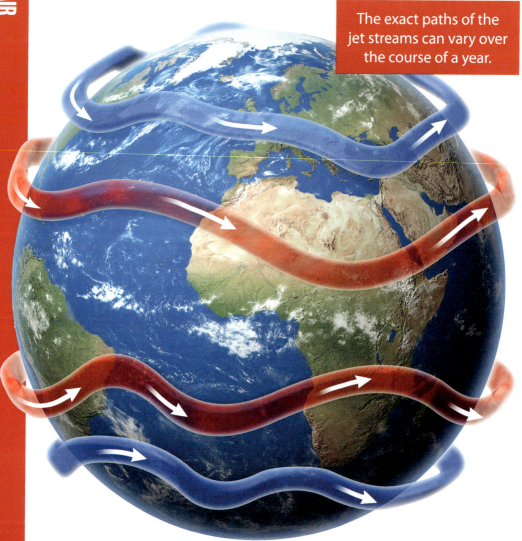

The exact paths of the jet streams can vary over the course of a year.

Other planets have jet streams, too. A jet stream at Saturn's north pole forms the shape of a hexagon.

lower angle from Earth. The jet stream dips toward the equator. Meteorologists call this a trough.

Just as the locations of air masses create jet streams, the jet streams can affect air masses. The speed and movement of a jet stream can push air masses, moving warm and cold fronts around and causing changes in the weather. Meteorologists sometimes refer to jet streams as weather directors because of the effect they have on how weather acts.

THE CLIMATE IS CHANGING

Many human activities depend on the expected patterns of weather and climate in an area.

The weather created by all these processes follows a pattern over time that becomes known as the climate. Climate includes all the basic weather information about an area, such as how warm or cold it will be or how likely it is to rain or snow. Knowing an area's climate helps people make predictions about the weather for an area months in advance. It allows skiers to estimate when their favorite mountain will have the best snow for skiing. Farmers can plan the ideal time to plant or harvest their crops.

While climate changes much more slowly than weather, it does change. For example, looking back over thousands of years, scientists know that much of the northern half of Earth was once covered in ice. Many natural factors created this long-term climate change. As Earth's tilt and orbit changed slightly over time, northern areas got more direct sunlight. The Earth warmed up and the ice melted.

Past ice ages made Earth look much different than it does today.

THE CLIMATE IS CHANGING

Drilling for ice samples reveals a lot about the planet's past climate.

To learn what the weather was like thousands of years ago, scientists study things that were on Earth at the time. They dig up layers of rock and sediment at the bottoms of oceans and lakes. They drill into ice at Earth's poles. They study such things as tree rings and fossils. Scientists analyze clues that show how factors such as temperature, water, and wind created Earth's weather and climate in the past.

Scientists have discovered that changes in the climate can be caused by a number of different things. Some of them happen naturally. Some of them happen because of human actions. Scientists study all these things to understand how the climate has changed in the past, how it is changing today, and how it will continue to change in the future.

A changing climate threatens the survival of many species.

NATURAL CAUSES OF A CHANGING CLIMATE

The sun is the main source of energy for Earth's weather, and the amount of energy it releases changes over time. This can have an effect on the planet's climate. Changes in Earth's position can change the climate too. Earth rotates on a tilted axis, and it also orbits around the sun. These constant shifts in Earth's position and angle with regard to the sun can affect the atmosphere.

Earth's motion over time influences the planet's climate.

The shifting of continents can change the climate in those regions.

Some natural factors that can change Earth's climate come from within the planet. Earth's landmasses sit on giant slabs of rock called tectonic plates. These plates move and shift over time. Over many millions of years, they can move an area to a new climate. For example, about 300 million years ago the land that is now Great Britain was near the equator. The movement of tectonic plates brought it to its present position farther north.

NATURAL CAUSES OF A CHANGING CLIMATE

There is another way tectonic plates can affect the climate. When these plates move, they can form volcanoes. These are places where hot, melted rock from deep inside the planet rises to the surface. A volcanic eruption sends large amounts of dust and rock into the atmosphere. These materials may linger in the atmosphere for weeks. They block some of the sun's light, reducing the solar energy that reaches the surface. This can cool Earth's temperature. Volcanoes also release gases that trap heat in the atmosphere. This can cause long-term warming.

The effects of volcanic activity are visible from space.

A volcano's release of gas and dust into the atmosphere can block sunlight and change the climate.

NATURAL CAUSES OF A CHANGING CLIMATE

One rare cause of climate change is an asteroid strike. Asteroids are rocks that drift through space. Many of them come near Earth, but most small ones burn up harmlessly in the atmosphere. If a large one hits the planet, it could send

Asteroid strikes can have catastrophic effects on the planet and its climate.

large clouds of dust into the air, similar to volcanoes. Scientists believe that this may have happened in the past. An asteroid that hit Central America 66 million years ago may have triggered climate changes that helped kill off the dinosaurs.

HUMAN CAUSES OF CLIMATE CHANGE

Many changes to Earth's climate are the result of natural causes. However, scientists have also found that some things people do affect Earth's climate. Many of these things increase the amount of greenhouse gases in the atmosphere. The gases in Earth's atmosphere affect how much of the sun's energy gets through to the planet. Some of these gases trap heat in the atmosphere, preventing it from reflecting back into space. This has the effect of warming the planet over time. These gases are known as greenhouse gases.

Just as a glass greenhouse traps heat inside it, greenhouse gases trap the sun's heat in the atmosphere.

Sea level rise could threaten island inhabitants.

When the temperature warms as a result of greenhouse gases, the flow of air currents and the jet stream can change. This can lead to changes in the weather. It can also warm up areas that are covered in ice, leading to melting. When ice on the land melts, it can drain into the sea and gradually raise the water level of the oceans.

The main greenhouse gases are water vapor, carbon dioxide, methane, nitrous oxide, and ozone. All of these can be produced by natural processes. For example, people and animals breathe out carbon dioxide. Animals release methane as part of the process of digesting food. Volcanoes can release some greenhouse gases into the atmosphere.

HUMAN CAUSES OF CLIMATE CHANGE

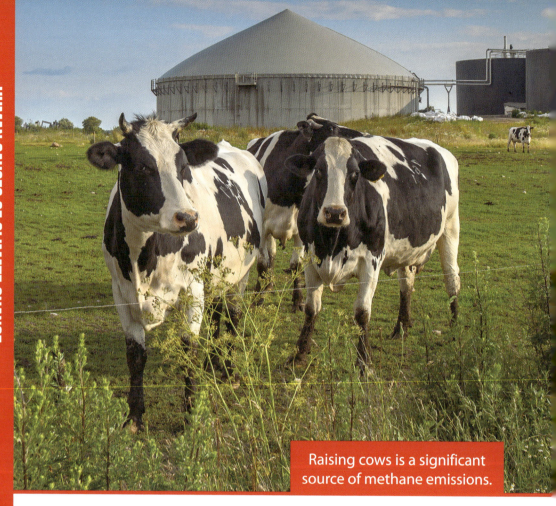

Raising cows is a significant source of methane emissions.

But human activity can dramatically increase the emission of greenhouse gases. Industrialized countries with many big cities, power plants, factories, and vehicles use a lot of energy from fossil fuels. These are the most common sources of energy on the planet. They are the energy-rich remains of living things that died millions of years ago and turned into substances such as coal, oil, and natural gas through geological processes. These fuels contain carbon, and when they are burned for energy, carbon dioxide is released into the atmosphere. Greenhouse gases act like a blanket that holds in heat from the sun. This effect warms the planet's average temperature over time. This can change the patterns of the convection process, air currents, and the jet streams, causing significant shifts in weather and climate.

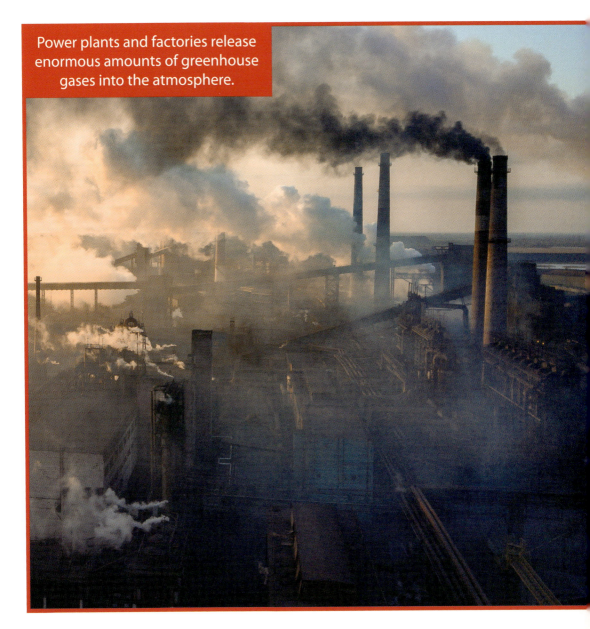

Power plants and factories release enormous amounts of greenhouse gases into the atmosphere.

HUMAN CAUSES OF CLIMATE CHANGE

Fossil fuels are a major factor in human-caused climate change, but people affect the climate in other ways too. Trees and plants take in carbon dioxide and give off oxygen. As a result, when people clear forests to build cities, more of this greenhouse gas stays in the atmosphere. This warms the planet.

Clearing forests makes it harder to counter the buildup of greenhouse gases in the atmosphere.

A changing climate affects how people live. Hotter temperatures can make some areas more difficult to live in. Changing weather patterns can bring too much or too little rain to a region. Rising seas can flood islands and coastlines. Extreme weather conditions, such as strong storms and long droughts, can become more common.

WEATHER PHENOMENA

Weather is caused by factors that can be hard to see with the naked eye, such as jet streams, solar energy, and moving masses of air. When people think of the weather, they likely think of the parts of weather that are visible from the ground in

Weather has a significant influence on daily life.

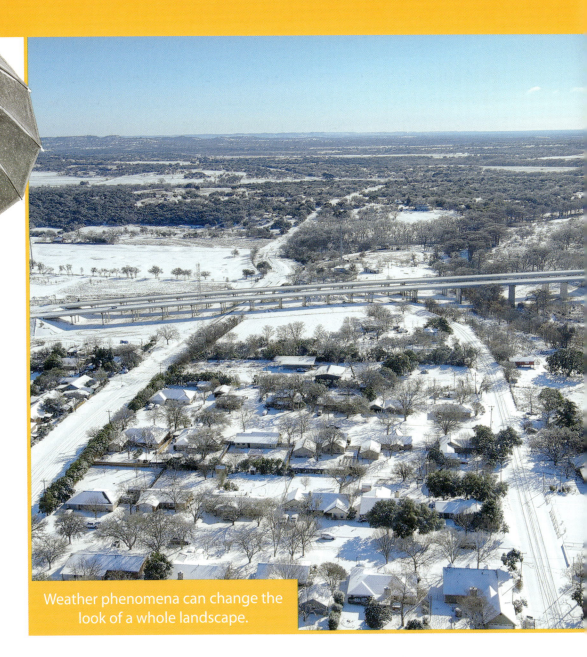

Weather phenomena can change the look of a whole landscape.

everyday life. They might think of things like clouds, rain, snow, and other weather events that people can observe. These are known as weather phenomena.

CLOUDS

Clouds are a very common type of weather phenomena. The air that surrounds Earth includes water vapor, which is the gas form of water. The vapor is made up of tiny drops of water. As the air gets warmer, it rises as a warm air mass. This causes the tiny drops to come together to form larger drops. Eventually those drops get big enough to reflect sunlight. This is what people see as clouds.

No two clouds are exactly alike. However, there are some similarities in how they look and act. Meteorologists can tell a lot about the weather from looking at the kinds of clouds in the sky. They group clouds in ten main types. These types are based on what the clouds look like and where they are in the atmosphere. Each kind has its own effect on weather. In 1803, an English pharmacist and amateur meteorologist named Luke

Clouds typically float thousands of feet above ground level.

Howard described and named the characteristics of clouds in his book, *Essay on the Modifications of Clouds*. Meteorologists around the world still use his terms today.

Three types of clouds are found high in the atmosphere at around 20,000 feet (6,100 m). They are called cirrus, cirrocumulus, and cirrostratus clouds. Cirrus clouds are fine, thin clouds that usually form when there is not enough water vapor in the air to form bigger clouds closer to the ground. They often mean calm, dry weather. Cirrocumulus clouds are so high in the atmosphere that the water vapor freezes into ice crystals. These crystals form lots of very small clusters in patterns that resemble honeycombs or fish scales. They do not usually affect the weather, but the conditions that form

Luke Howard sketched clouds as he worked to categorize the many types he saw in the sky.

Cirrus clouds have a wispy appearance.

them can lead to storms. Cirrostratus clouds are also made up of ice crystals. They form in an almost invisible curtain that sometimes reflects light to make a halo around the sun or the moon. These clouds often mean it will rain soon.

Other types of clouds with more impact on weather form lower in the atmosphere. At the midlevel—between 6,500 feet and 20,000 feet (1,980 and 6,100 m)—there are three main types of clouds. They are called altocumulus, altostratus, and nimbostratus clouds. Altocumulus clouds are made up of rounded clumps. They form near mountains when other clouds break up, or when rising warm air with a lot of water vapor bumps into cooler air. These clouds are made of a mixture of ice and water. They can cause rain, but it rarely reaches the ground, instead evaporating before falling to Earth. Altostratus clouds are made of ice and water. They often form when cirrostratus

clouds drop down from higher in the atmosphere. Like cirrostratus clouds, they have the appearance of a thin curtain or sheet that lets light through. They do not cause weather but often turn into nimbostratus clouds. Nimbostratus clouds are weather makers. Unlike most other clouds that are white or light in color, nimbostratus clouds form in thick, gray bands that block sunlight. These are the clouds that cause rain and snow.

Nimbostratus clouds have a distinctive dark color.

Four types of clouds are found closest to Earth, at around 1,200 to 6,500 feet (370 to 1,980 m). Some of these clouds indicate what kind of weather is coming. Others are the sources of rain, snow, and other precipitation. These clouds are cumulus, stratus, stratocumulus, and cumulonimbus clouds. Stratus clouds are very close to Earth. Sometimes they are right at the ground. They can be white or gray and form in a smooth layer, like a blanket just above Earth's surface. They form in calm conditions.

CLOUDS

Sometimes they cause light rain or snow. Stratocumulus clouds form when stratus clouds break up. They form into white or gray patches or bunches of clouds. This often happens when a front is approaching, so stratocumulus clouds indicate that the weather is about to change. Cumulus clouds are puffy clouds that resemble cotton balls or cauliflower. These are the kinds of clouds seen on sunny days. However, in the right conditions, they can turn into cumulonimbus clouds. Cumulonimbus clouds are tall, towering clouds, usually gray in color and flat on top. If there is a lot of water vapor in the air, the ground is very hot, or a strong cold front arrives in an area, cumulus clouds can become cumulonimbus clouds. These clouds are present in thunderstorms. They are sometimes called thunderclouds.

Clouds can change from one type to another. They are affected by the movement of cold and warm air masses. Changes in temperature can also change clouds. So can changes in the amount of water in the air.

Clouds play an important role in both weather and climate.

Cumulonimbus clouds can extend high into the atmosphere.

CLOUDS

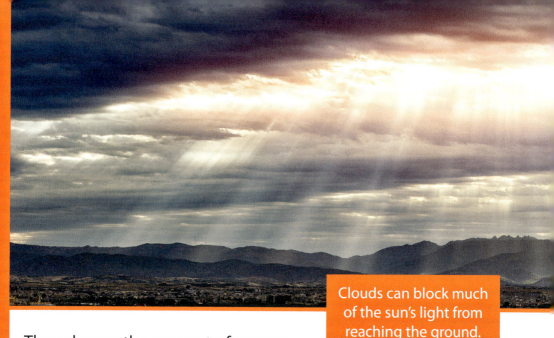

Clouds can block much of the sun's light from reaching the ground.

They change the amount of energy from the sun that reaches the ground. They also change how much and how fast heat moves from the ground into the atmosphere. Sometimes clouds reflect the sun's energy away from Earth. This makes things cooler on the surface below. Clouds can also absorb the heat that rises from Earth's surface. This heat is then either sent back to the surface or sent out into space. In these ways, clouds help to control the temperature on Earth.

Clouds also help to control the moisture levels in the atmosphere and on the surface of Earth. Clouds are made up of water vapor or water that has turned to ice. The water vapor comes from evaporation on Earth's surface. Evaporation is the process of a liquid turning into a gas. It can be caused by heat, temperature changes, and the action of wind. The water vapor from evaporation builds up in the clouds until there is too much moisture for the clouds to hold. Then it becomes precipitation. This movement of water between the surface and the atmosphere is known as the water cycle.

Clouds play a vital role in the water cycle, storing water and releasing it as rain.

PRECIPITATION

The cold air high above the ground helps turn a cloud's water vapor into precipitation.

Precipitation is water that falls from clouds to the ground. As water in the clouds builds up, it becomes heavy enough that gravity pulls it downward. It falls in one of three main forms: rain, snow, or other frozen precipitation.

Most of the precipitation that reaches Earth's surface is rain. Raindrops form when tiny amounts of moisture rise high above Earth as water vapor. Cooler air at high altitudes changes the water vapor back into liquid water. If enough of this water comes together, it turns into droplets and falls from the clouds.

Whether these droplets fall as rain or snow depends on the temperature closer to the surface. If it is warm, the droplets will stay in liquid form and fall as rain. If the temperature on the ground is below freezing, or 32 degrees Fahrenheit (0°C), the falling water will become snow or another form of freezing precipitation.

Each type of precipitation has its own characteristics. These characteristics depend on the temperature in the air and on the ground. They also depend on the humidity. Humidity is the measure of the amount of water vapor in the air. When there is a lot of water vapor, the humidity is high. When there is not much water vapor, the humidity is low.

Sometimes rain falls from clouds that do not block the sun, resulting in what is known as a sun shower.

BASIC TYPES OF PRECIPITATION

Rain falls from cumulus or stratus clouds. The clouds holding the most water vapor are dark. The water vapor blocks more sunlight, so the cloud looks thicker and darker. This is why gray clouds are often associated with rainfall.

Dark clouds are heavy with high amounts of water vapor.

Heavy rains make it challenging to get around outdoors.

Rain can fall in different ways. Sometimes the raindrops are small and light. This is often called a drizzle or a rain shower. Other times, the rain falls hard and fast in a downpour. The difference in falling rain varies based on the temperature and humidity of the air mass.

Cool air masses move more slowly and hold less water vapor. This means that smaller drops form and do not have to fight a strong air current to fall. This allows for a gentler rain or drizzle. Warm air masses move faster, and the clouds in them

BASIC TYPES OF PRECIPITATION

can hold much more water vapor. The stronger air currents hold the water vapor up in the sky for a longer time, so the droplets grow much bigger. When the air cannot hold them up any more, they fall hard and fast.

When the air close to the ground is at or below freezing temperature, snow can fall. Snow happens because water has an unusual property. Instead of getting smaller when it gets cold, it gets bigger. It turns into a snowflake, which is a crystal

The specific shape of the six-sided crystal varies from snowflake to snowflake.

with six sides. These crystals form around a smaller particle of ice or dirt. Snowflakes may look white, but they are actually clear. The ice crystals that form them reflect light in a way that makes them look white.

Snow almost always falls from stratus clouds, which are more likely to form in cooler temperatures. The clouds are often low in the atmosphere and thick with moisture, so they are usually gray in appearance. Sometimes, though, snow can fall from cumulus clouds. When this happens, it is because areas of low pressure have pushed more air up into the atmosphere. These storms usually produce higher amounts of snowfall.

Several inches of snow may accumulate from a single snowfall.

Rainwater generally washes away into the soil, but snow can accumulate on the ground in large amounts. The same amount of precipitation that would make 1 inch (2.54 cm) of

BASIC TYPES OF PRECIPITATION

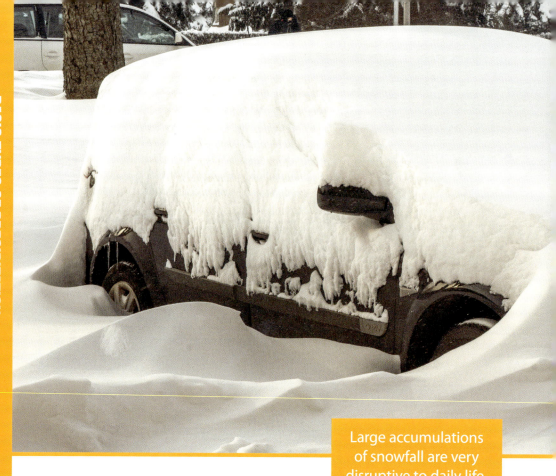

Large accumulations of snowfall are very disruptive to daily life.

rain would make 10 inches (25 cm) of snow. Accumulated snow can be used for recreation, such as skiing or snowshoeing. But it can also disrupt movement on roads and sidewalks.

Snow is a common form of frozen precipitation. But weather conditions can create other types as well. These include hail, freezing rain, sleet, and graupel.

Even though it is a frozen form of precipitation, hail happens only in warm weather. It forms in cumulonimbus clouds. Water drops start to fall but are pushed back up into cooler air by the strong winds of a thunderstorm. This allows another layer of water to freeze on the drop. The process repeats until the raindrop has become a chunk of ice that is heavy enough that the winds can no longer push it up. Then it falls as a hailstone.

The other types of freezing precipitation—freezing rain, sleet, and graupel—all form during warm fronts. This happens when warm air passes cold air. These types of precipitation usually come from stratus clouds.

Hail can grow large enough that it damages cars and roofs.

BASIC TYPES OF PRECIPITATION

Freezing rain happens when rain falling from warmer air masses runs into colder air near the ground. If it does not run into an ice crystal or particle of dirt to form a snowflake, it stays in liquid form. Once it lands on a cold surface, it freezes. Freezing rain can be very hard to see. It often makes the ground look like it is just wet, but it is extremely slippery. This makes walking or driving dangerous. Freezing rain also creates problems when it coats power lines and tree branches. Just a small amount of freezing rain can be heavy enough to pull branches down, causing power outages and damage to buildings.

Freezing rain coats objects and surfaces with a thin layer of ice.

Sleet can leave sidewalks dangerously slick.

Sleet is similar to freezing rain, but it runs into cold air a little farther from the surface. This allows the raindrops to form a frozen outer shell. Sometimes sleet forms from snow that starts to melt as it falls but is refrozen when it falls through cold air near the ground. It can be hard to tell sleet from rain or freezing rain when it is falling. However, sleet usually falls as small pellets that bounce on the ground. These often melt and then refreeze, making sidewalks and roads slippery and dangerous.

BASIC TYPES OF PRECIPITATION

Graupel is softer than hail and is less damaging when it falls.

Graupel is formed when snow falls through very cold rain. The rain collects on the snow. This process, called riming, forms soft, rounded chunks that are generally 0.08 to 0.2 inches (2 to 5 mm) wide. While falling hail is hard and loud, falling graupel is much quieter. Chunks of it can often be squished between fingers, and it is not as dangerous as hail, sleet, or freezing rain. Graupel is sometimes referred to as snow pellets or soft hail.

All kinds of precipitation play a role in the water cycle, returning water from clouds to the ground. They can be helpful or harmful. Rain feeds crops, while hail can damage them. Each kind of precipitation can also be disruptive to human activities.

Rainfall and other forms of precipitation are important to life on Earth.

DEW, FROST, AND FOG

Drops of dew are often seen on blades of grass.

Sometimes moisture in the air causes weather phenomena other than precipitation. These phenomena include dew, frost, and fog. They result from moisture in the air below the clouds, and they do not fall from clouds, as precipitation does.

Dew and frost form when warm air near the ground cools down. The cooler air cannot hold as much water vapor. The water vapor in the air turns into drops of liquid water that appear on the ground and other surfaces. If the temperature at ground level is above freezing, the water will stay in liquid form. This is known as dew. If the temperature on the ground is below freezing, the water droplets will freeze and turn into ice crystals. This is called frost. Frost can be lethal to growing plants.

Fog is actually a very low stratus cloud. Several types of fog can form, based on the conditions that exist near the ground. Radiation fog forms when ground heat rises up overnight, causing the ground to become cooler. The moisture in the air condenses, or gets denser, and forms a very low cloud. Advection fog is seen along coastlines. Warmer air currents moving over cold air cause the air to condense and form low clouds right at ground level. Evaporation fog usually forms over

Farmers may cover their crops to protect them from frost.

DEW, FROST, AND FOG

bodies of water, such as lakes, rivers, and oceans. It happens when the water is warmer than the air above it. This causes the water in the air to condense into fog. Finally, valley fog is formed by the way mountains and valleys affect the flow of

air currents. Air that runs into mountains becomes filled with water vapor and forms a low cloud. When cold air gets trapped in the valleys between mountains, this air can also collect enough water vapor to form fog.

Fog may form in a landscape's low areas.

OTHER WEATHER PHENOMENA

The combination of water vapor, the actions of air masses, and temperature create other weather phenomena in the sky. Some are dangerous, such as lightning. Others, such as rainbows, are beautiful. Each happens for a different reason and can reveal a lot about conditions in the atmosphere.

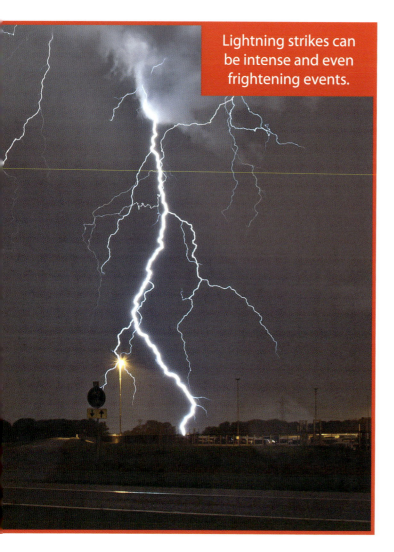

Lightning strikes can be intense and even frightening events.

Lightning is one of the most spectacular displays of weather. It is also one of the most dangerous. It can kill or injure people, destroy property, and start fires. Lightning is electricity that forms in thunderclouds, also known as cumulonimbus clouds. The warm air masses with these clouds move upward at around 60 miles per hour (97 kmh).

Ice crystals in a cloud move around

The interactions between electrical charges in clouds and the ground results in lightning.

rapidly and collide with each other. The ice crystals have negatively charged particles called electrons on them. These particles are knocked off by the collisions. The electric charges inside the cloud become separated. The top of the cloud has a positive charge, while the bottom has a negative charge. The ground below has a positive charge. When the cloud's negative charge gets big enough, a negative charge comes down from the cloud. When it meets a positive charge coming up from the ground, a lightning bolt happens.

    Some lightning stays in the clouds. This kind of lightning is called a cloud flash. Sometimes lightning leaves the clouds but stays high in the air. Other lightning stretches from the cloud toward Earth's surface. This is called cloud-to-ground lightning. This is the most dangerous form of lightning. Lightning that

OTHER WEATHER PHENOMENA

stays in the air is around five to ten times more common than cloud-to-ground lightning.

When lightning stretches toward the ground, it naturally seeks the path of least resistance. This means it travels along the fastest, easiest way to connect from its source in the clouds to the ground. Lightning usually strikes the tallest object in

Lightning may illuminate clouds without hitting the ground.

A lightning strike can cause extreme damage to a tree.

an area. This can be a tree or a tall building. It can also be a person standing out in the open.

Lightning is more likely to strike objects that are conductive. Conductive objects let electricity flow more easily. For instance, metal is more conductive than rubber or plastic. This is why power cords have metal inside to conduct electricity and plastic or rubber outside to keep the electricity safely inside.

OTHER WEATHER PHENOMENA

To stay safe from lightning, people in a thunderstorm should avoid being close to anything tall or metal and stay out of the water. Inside a building or a vehicle is the safest place to be when lightning is flashing.

Lightning also causes thunder. The energy of a lightning bolt creates a bright flash of light and a sudden burst of heat. The temperature of a lightning discharge can reach as high as 50,000 degrees Fahrenheit (27,800°C), far hotter than even lava from a volcano. This makes the air near the lightning discharge very hot. It expands very fast, and this expansion makes a noise that is heard as thunder.

Thunder is not dangerous by itself. However, it can warn of a thunderstorm nearby. If thunder is heard, it means lightning is happening. This is a good sign that it is time to seek shelter. Light moves

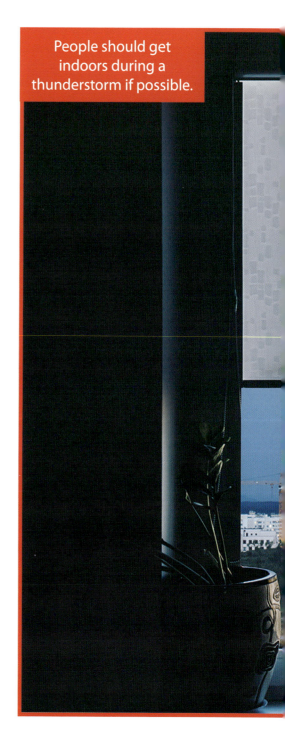

People should get indoors during a thunderstorm if possible.

OTHER WEATHER PHENOMENA

A nearby lightning strike is incredibly loud.

much faster than sound. This means that people hear thunder shortly after seeing the lightning bolt that caused it. It takes the sound of thunder about five seconds to travel one mile (1.6 km). People can use this fact to estimate how far away the lightning is.

Timing the gap between lightning and thunder can tell a person the rough distance to the lightning strike.

CLEAR-SKY PHENOMENA

Rainbows are among the most distinctive and striking clear-sky phenomena.

There are also several weather phenomena that do not happen during storms. Most are caused by the way sunlight reflects off water or ice. The best-known clear-sky phenomena are rainbows. Rainbows happen when sunlight reflects and refracts off water droplets high in the sky. Reflecting means that the sunlight bounces straight away from the droplets. Refracting means that the light bends and changes direction when it strikes the droplets.

As the sunlight reflects and refracts, the light is separated into different wavelengths. Each wavelength is a different color, and the order of the colors is always the same. This separated light is seen in the sky as a rainbow. Rainbows often happen when the sun comes out after a rainstorm because there are still a lot of water droplets in the atmosphere. Sometimes there is even enough that the light reflects and refracts twice. This results in two rainbows, one directly above the other, or a double rainbow. Rainbows usually appear as wide arcs from the ground, but they actually form full circles. This can usually be seen only from a high spot or an airplane.

In a double rainbow, the order of the colors in the second rainbow is reversed.

CLEAR-SKY PHENOMENA

Even when there is not enough water in the air to form a rainbow, sunlight reflects and refracts in the atmosphere. This creates the color of the sky. Blue waves of light are the shortest. They also scatter more easily. This is why the sky appears blue when the sun is high in the sky on a clear day. Red and yellow waves are longer and do not scatter as easily. When the sun is rising or setting, Earth's curvature lets these waves reach the surface more easily than the blue waves. This is why the sky looks red, yellow, and orange when the sun is rising or setting. They can also happen when something in the air makes the sunlight reflect and refract in an unusual way. Smoke from wildfires and ash from volcanos can cause red skies when they affect how the sunlight appears.

When the sun is low, the sky takes on a reddish color.

Greenish skies are linked to tornadoes.

The way the sun reflects and refracts off water in the air can change the color of the sky on cloudy days too. Sometimes sleet or freezing rain change how the sunlight is reflected and refracted. It blocks most of the colors except yellow, giving the sky a yellowish tint. Sometimes when severe storms are approaching, the sky turns green. Scientists are not sure exactly why this happens, but they think it has to do with ice in the clouds and the angle of the sun above the clouds.

LIGHT PHENOMENA

Some weather phenomena have to do with how the sun is seen from Earth. They are mostly caused by the sun's light reflecting and refracting off of clouds or ice crystals in the atmosphere. None of these are dangerous, but some are very pretty to see.

Sometimes it seems like the sun or the moon has a shimmering band of light around it. This happens when the light is reflected and refracted off thin bands

Thin clouds can produce a visible lunar corona.

A 22-degree halo was visible around the sun in Moscow, Russia, in late December 2021.

of stratus or cumulus clouds. The disc of light that appears is called a corona. These features are more often visible around the moon because they contrast against the dark night sky.

A phenomenon similar to a corona is called the 22-degree halo. It gets this name because it is found at an angle of 22 degrees from the center of the sun or, more often, the moon. A halo is caused by light interacting with ice crystals in the atmosphere. This causes what looks like a rainbow around the sun or moon. Halos happen more often in cold weather that allows ice crystals to form.

LIGHT PHENOMENA

In a moon dog, faint bright spots appear on either side of the moon.

A sun dog or moon dog is similar to a 22-degree halo. Light reflected off ice crystals creates what looks like a reflection of either the sun or the moon that appears 22 degrees away from the actual sun or moon. Sun dogs are more common because the sun is brighter. Like the 22-degree halo, sun and moon dogs appear most often in cold weather.

A sun pillar looks like a tower of light rising up above the sun. This phenomenon usually happens when the sun is rising or setting. The sun's light reflects and refracts off of ice crystals and high clouds. This creates a tall stream of light above the sun.

In a sun pillar, a tall column of light appears to rise from the sun when it is low on the horizon.

LIGHT PHENOMENA

The northern lights form a stunning display in the night sky.

    The most spectacular of the light phenomena caused by the sun is probably the aurora borealis, commonly known as the northern lights. This phenomenon is caused not by the sun's light but by a stream of charged particles the sun gives off, called solar wind. When the solar wind interacts with the upper atmosphere, a special kind of light show happens. This is the result of ionization, or the process of adding or removing electrons from an atom. The solar wind creates beautiful displays of bright colors in the atmosphere. The northern lights are most visible in locations closer to the North Pole. They are easiest to see in a clear night sky. The same phenomenon is known as the aurora australis, or the southern lights, when it occurs in the southern hemisphere.

Researchers launch rockets into an aurora to study the phenomenon.

WEATHER FORECASTING

Today's meteorologists use sophisticated equipment to track and predict the weather.

Observing the current weather is one thing. Being able to predict what weather will happen in a few hours, days, or even weeks can be extremely challenging. This is the goal of a branch of science called meteorology. The word *meteorology* comes from the Greek word *meteoros*, meaning "in the air," and the Greek word *logia*, meaning "to discuss, study, or explain." Meteorology is the science and study of Earth's atmosphere, weather, and climate. The ancient Greeks are credited with beginning the science of meteorology around 350 BCE.

The scientists who are trained in this field are called meteorologists. They usually have at least one college degree in meteorology or related sciences and are trained to use scientific equipment and methods to study and predict weather. In some cases, people who have specialized training through the military or another organization are also called meteorologists.

All weather forecasting is done by meteorologists. Sometimes weather reporters will appear on television to report what the weather will be. They will use information prepared by

Specialized meteorologists work for the US military.

WEATHER FORECASTING

Weather reporters play an important role in spreading weather information to the public.

meteorologists, but the weather reporters may or may not be actual meteorologists themselves.

Ancient people studied the sky and tried to predict the weather. However, it was not until the middle of the 1800s that people consistently used tools for weather forecasting. There are several basic tools that are still used to forecast weather today. One is the thermometer, which is used to measure temperature. Another is the barometer, which measures atmospheric pressure. A barometer has a column of

mercury, air, or water inside. By measuring how much air is pressing down on the contents of this column, people can determine the atmospheric pressure. An anemometer is used to measure wind speed. This device usually includes a series of cups that catch the wind and spin around a central point. People can measure how fast the cups spin to determine the wind speed.

An anemometer is a simple but useful tool for determining wind conditions.

WEATHER FORECASTING

These tools are inexpensive and easy to get. Many amateur weather fans use them to determine and record the atmospheric conditions where they live. There are also special weather tools that are usually used only by professional meteorologists. Hygrometers measure humidity, or the amount of water in the air. Pyranometers measure solar energy. Ceilometers measure how high clouds are in the sky. Computerized collection systems gather information from multiple thermometers, barometers, and anemometers, giving meteorologists access to more information quickly.

Ceilometers shine lasers upward and sense the light that bounces back, allowing them to determine the height of clouds.

90

More complex and expensive gear is usually used by governments or large organizations. Radar sends radio waves into the atmosphere. The waves bounce off clouds, air masses, and other weather phenomena. The radar equipment senses the reflected waves to determine the shape, distance, and size of these objects. Weather satellites are launched into Earth orbit to study the planet's atmosphere from above. They are able to constantly monitor solar energy, the atmosphere, and more. They provide much more information than can be collected by land-based equipment. Computer models allow meteorologists to detect patterns in air currents, fronts, storms, and other weather factors. They take in a wide variety of weather data and then use this information to predict how weather changes are likely to unfold over the following hours, days, and weeks. For example, a hurricane computer model tries to determine the most likely future path of the storm.

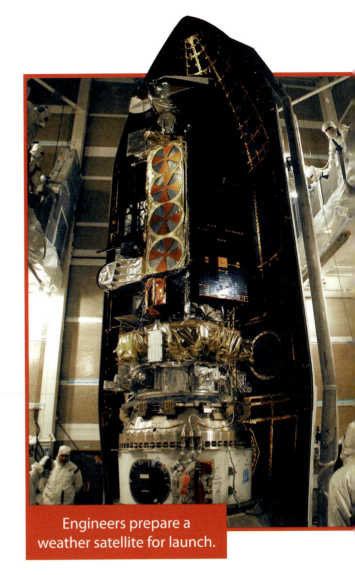

Engineers prepare a weather satellite for launch.

WEATHER FORECASTING

Weather forecasts can help people plan their everyday lives. People may use them to decide whether to wear shorts, carry an umbrella, or pack a coat for their vacation. But these forecasts can also be literal life savers. The ability to predict extreme weather, such as thunderstorms, blizzards, hurricanes, and tornadoes, helps to protect lives and property. Meteorologists share different types of information about these events to help the public prepare for potentially devastating weather occurrences.

These weather notifications generally fall into a few separate categories. A watch lets people know that there is the possibility of a weather event, such as a storm. An advisory is

In addition to warning viewers about dangerous storms, weather reporters may follow the storms and report live from the scene.

The immense damage that storms cause makes a meteorologist's warnings extremely important.

more urgent. It means that the conditions for a severe weather event to happen have been observed in a particular area. A warning is the most urgent message issued by meteorologists. It means that the severe weather has already started and may be approaching. Warnings are issued for such events as thunderstorms, flash floods, tornadoes, winter storms, and blizzards. One of a meteorologist's most important jobs is to help people prepare for these kinds of extreme weather events.

EXTREME STORMS:
WHAT IS EXTREME WEATHER?

Weather happens everywhere on Earth every day. Sunny days, cold days, rainy days, and dry days are all part of the normal weather patterns across the globe. Sometimes, though, the weather is much more severe. Rain may fall hard for hours or days, leading to flooding. Snowfall may be measured in feet, burying cars. Winds may blow hard enough to take down trees or buildings. Weather that has the capability to harm people, nature, or property is often referred to as extreme weather.

Extreme weather goes beyond what is normally seen for that type of event in a given area. To determine how extreme an event is, meteorologists can look at information about the past weather in the area and determine how likely a certain weather event is to happen there. A rare event may be described as a historic blizzard or a 100-year flood. This means that a flood of that severity is expected to occur just once every 100 years.

Flooded roads are among the many kinds of dangerous conditions that can be caused by severe storms.

EXTREME STORMS: WHAT IS EXTREME WEATHER?

Extreme storms can cause widespread devastation.

    A weather event that is extreme in one area might not be extreme in another. For example, it would not be unusual for some cities in the northern United States to see a foot (30.5 cm) of snowfall in a storm. A storm like this would not be considered an extreme event. However, a storm that left a foot of snow on the ground in Florida would be highly unusual and potentially dangerous. That's because people in that area may not be familiar with how to handle such a weather event. Or the state may not have the tools—such as snowplows—to properly deal with the weather.

Extreme weather may put lives in danger or cause significant damage. Some kinds of events, such as floods, tornadoes, and hurricanes, might be considered extreme no matter where they happen. They can destroy an area in minutes or hours.

Texas was hit by a rare snowstorm in early 2021.

EXTREME STORMS: WHAT IS EXTREME WEATHER?

Extreme weather is such a big risk to life and property that governments create special agencies to track and predict it. In the United States, this includes the National Weather Service (NWS), which is run by the National Oceanic and Atmospheric Administration (NOAA). Other agencies within the United States study, monitor, and predict weather at the national, state, and local levels. Other countries have their own weather services.

The NWS is the main source for official weather forecasts in the United States. It also runs a website, weather.gov, that includes images of radar and satellite maps. The website features information about stream and river levels. This allows anyone to monitor the potential for floods.

The National Weather Service is part of the National Oceanic and Atmospheric Administration.

Experts at the National Hurricane Center track various sources of data to make their predictions.

NOAA runs three other special weather centers. The Storm Prediction Center (SPC) monitors severe storms and tornadoes. The Weather Prediction Center (WPC) monitors precipitation across the United States. The National Hurricane Center (NHC) watches the development of tropical storms.

All of these organizations use computer modeling, satellite imagery, and other state-of-the art technology to monitor and track storms. They can predict many regular and extreme weather events hours or even days before they arrive. This helps save thousands of lives each year. It allows people to take steps to limit property damage as well.

EXTREME STORMS: WHAT IS EXTREME WEATHER?

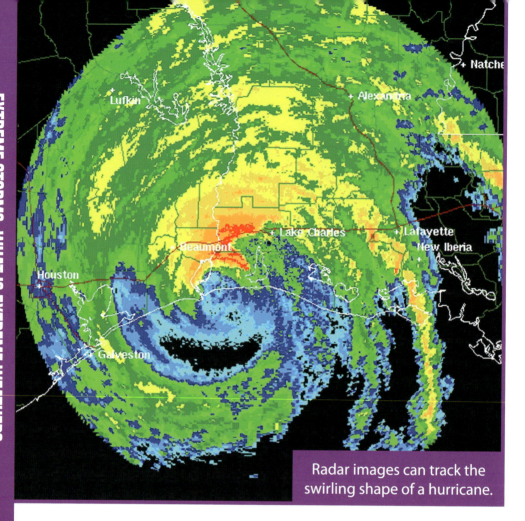

Radar images can track the swirling shape of a hurricane.

Forecasting technology has improved dramatically over the past 200 years. In the 1800s, people were much more at the mercy of weather than they are today. Extreme storms often caught people by surprise. The only available forecasters were volunteers. They relied on observations using basic equipment and their own knowledge of past weather events. Then the telegraph system spread across the country. People could send simple messages from city to city almost instantly. For the first time, people in one area were able to warn others about weather headed in their direction. These were the first real forecasts.

In 1870, the US Army Signal Service's Division of Telegrams and Reports for the Benefit of Commerce was started. This division was responsible for weather forecasting until 1890. That's when a new nonmilitary organization, the US Weather Bureau, was created. The bureau was given the job of tracking and forecasting weather. It was renamed the NWS in 1970.

The invention of the telegraph allowed people to send information, including weather data, across vast distances almost instantly.

EXTREME STORMS: WHAT IS EXTREME WEATHER?

A Weather Bureau staff member uses equipment to track weather balloons in the 1940s.

Extreme weather takes a number of different forms. Some of these events happen more often when it is warmer or colder. Others are more common in certain parts of the world compared with other regions. All of them present some danger to people. Knowing about them can help people prepare and be safe.

Being aware of upcoming flood conditions gives people a chance to set up sandbags to limit the damage.

THUNDERSTORMS

Thunderstorms are a common type of weather that can sometimes become extreme. It is estimated that more than 16 million thunderstorms happen around the world each year. There may be as many as 2,000 thunderstorms going on around the world at any given time. They happen most often in the afternoon and evening during the summer and spring. However, they can happen anywhere and at any time if the conditions are right. The main conditions for a thunderstorm are warm air on the ground that rises, air currents that nudge the warm air upward, and a lot of water vapor in the air.

Some thunderstorms are relatively mild, but others result in significant destruction.

The simplest definition of a thunderstorm is a storm in which thunder is heard. Because thunder is caused by lightning, this means all thunderstorms have lightning. Therefore, all thunderstorms can be considered dangerous. But only some of them are classified as severe storms. A thunderstorm is considered severe if it meets one or more conditions. The first condition is that it has wind gusts greater than 50 knots, or 57.5 miles per hour (92.5 kmh). The second is that it produces hail that is more than 1 inch (2.54 cm) wide. And the third is that it results in one or more tornadoes.

THUNDERSTORMS

Severe thunderstorms can cause many types of damage. Lightning can injure or kill people. Sometimes it sets buildings, trees, or grass on fire. Thunderstorms sometimes produce large hail. This can damage property and cause injuries. Thunderstorms with high winds can blow down trees. High winds can also cause damage to buildings or take down power lines. Sometimes the rain from thunderstorms is so intense and heavy that it causes flash flooding.

Large hail is one common feature of severe thunderstorms.

Fallen trees are capable of causing considerable damage.

Weather experts track the conditions that lead to thunderstorms. They watch for cumulus clouds that get pushed upward by an updraft of rising warm air. By monitoring the air currents, the temperature, and the amount of water vapor in the air, meteorologists can determine how dangerous a storm will be. They issue thunderstorm watches and warnings.

THUNDERSTORMS

Radar lets meteorologists figure out the size and power of a thunderstorm.

    Thunderstorms come with a built-in warning system in the thunder and lightning they produce. The best way to stay safe in a thunderstorm is to pay attention. People should listen for thunder. They should pay attention to weather reports in case meteorologists issue watches and warnings. They should get inside and stay there during storms to be safe from lightning and hail. If people are outdoors and cannot seek shelter, they should stay away from tall objects and bodies of water that attract lightning.

Experts say that being inside a car during a lightning storm is safer than being outdoors.

FLOODS

Floods are the most common natural disasters in the United States and in many other parts of the world. They happen when water fills an area that is not normally covered by water. Some floods involve very deep water. Other floods are as shallow as a few inches. Almost any flood can cause death, injury, and property damage.

Flooding often happens when large amounts of rain fall, causing streams, rivers, and lakes to overflow beyond their boundaries. These boundaries can be the natural banks and shores of the waterways. They can also be human-made boundaries, such as levees, dams, and drainage systems. A levee is an embankment made of dirt, rock, or concrete. It is

Major floods can leave a community's roadways totally inaccessible.

Drainage systems are meant to prevent flooding.

built alongside a waterway to make its natural bank higher. This helps prevent flooding. They are also known as dikes or floodbanks. A dam is a structure built across a stream or river to hold back and control the flow of water. It allows people to collect water for future use or for recreational purposes. It may also be used to produce electricity by running the collected water through power-generating turbines. Dam floods can be catastrophic. In 1889, a dam near Johnstown, Pennsylvania, failed because of poor construction and heavy rain. Nearly 2,000 buildings were destroyed and 2,200 people were killed by the sudden gush of water.

A drainage system is a set of pipes, trenches, and other devices. It helps prevent water from collecting or flooding an area. These systems can be under or above ground.

FLOODS

Storm surges directly threaten buildings along the shore.

When it rains hard for a long period of time, rainwater can overwhelm these human-made boundaries. Flooding frequently follows hurricanes, for example. Some of this flooding is caused by storm surges. Storm surges happen during hurricanes. The storm makes the sea level rise, and ocean waters move onto the shore. This threatens homes and businesses in coastal areas.

Sometimes other factors increase the likelihood of flooding. For instance, seasonal flooding occurs in spring when waterways fill with melted snow and ice. This can be made worse by rainstorms in spring and early summer.

In the past, people could predict a flood only if they were able to directly observe the water rising. Now, scientists use stream gauges and other devices in rivers and other bodies of water. These gauges record the amount of water present and how much it increases or decreases. This information is used to monitor water level increases that could lead to flooding.

Gauges help scientists track the water level in rivers that are at risk of flooding.

FLOODS

Stream gauges and weather forecasts for incoming storms allow meteorologists to predict this type of flooding days in advance. Another type of flooding happens faster and gives less notice. Sometimes a storm suddenly drops a large amount of rain in a short period. This can overwhelm storm drainage systems, streams, and rivers, causing them to spill water onto land. These types of floods are known as flash floods. They are especially dangerous when the water covers roads and bridges. Meteorologists track and predict flash floods by monitoring thunderstorms and hurricanes that could produce a lot of rain.

Flash floods may cover roads, stranding motorists.

Rescuers may use boats to help people in the aftermath of a severe flood.

    Staying safe from floods involves both advance planning and immediate action when watches and warnings are issued. People who live in areas with frequent flooding should have a plan in place for where they will go if flooding is predicted. This plan should include having supplies of food, water, clothing, medicine, and other necessities while evacuating.

    If a flood watch is issued, people should prepare to evacuate. Once a warning is issued, people should listen to the recommendations of authorities. People may need to leave the area and go to a safe place on higher ground.

    It's important to use caution when traveling. Never walk or drive onto a flooded road. A flash flood with as little as 6 inches (15.2 cm) of water can have a current that moves fast enough to knock people off their feet. One foot (30.5 cm) of moving floodwater is enough to carry a car off a road. People should not go back into the flooded area until officials say it is safe. They should follow the advice of local authorities to stay safe from danger in the flood's aftermath.

HURRICANES

Flooding often results from hurricanes. Hurricanes are large tropical storm systems. They may be 500 miles (805 km) wide and reach 10 miles (16 km) from ground to sky. The storm system rotates like a giant top around a low-pressure area. This low-pressure area causes heavy rains and winds ranging from 74 to more than 157 miles per hour (119 to 253 kmh). When these storms reach land, they cause significant damage from rainfall, high winds, and flooding.

The swirling shape of a hurricane is so large that it is easily visible from the International Space Station.

Weather satellites tracked a major typhoon heading toward the Philippines in 2015.

The name *hurricane* is specific to a particular region. Large tropical storms that form in the North Atlantic and Northeast Pacific Oceans are called hurricanes. The same storm in the Northwest Pacific is called a typhoon. In the South Pacific and Indian Oceans, these storms are called cyclones. These names all refer to the same kind of storm.

Hurricanes start out over the ocean, where warm, moist air begins to rise higher into the atmosphere. Cooler air moves in to replace the warm air, and this convection process repeats until a large low-pressure area forms. This causes thunderstorms to develop. As the convection

HURRICANES

The interplay between warm and cool air leads to the powerful circular winds of a hurricane.

process continues, the storm grows larger and larger. When its wind speeds reach around 40 miles per hour (64 kmh), meteorologists call it a tropical storm. Once the winds reach at least 74 miles per hour (119 kmh), the storm is called a hurricane. Meteorologists classify hurricanes on a scale of one to five based on wind speed. This scale is known as the Saffir-Simpson Hurricane Wind Scale.

A category one storm has the lowest winds, but it is still a dangerous storm. Its wind speeds range from 74 to 95 miles per hour (119 to 153 kmh). These storms can cause damage to roofs and siding, break branches, and knock down power lines.

A category two storm has wind speeds of 96 to 110 miles per hour (155 to 177 kmh). It causes more significant damage to roofs and siding, uproots some trees, and tears down branches. This can result in blocked roads and downed power lines that take days to repair.

A category three storm has wind speeds of 111 to 129 miles per hour (179 to 208 kmh). It is considered a major hurricane. It is capable of causing hundreds of thousands, if not millions, of dollars in damage. Roofs may be ripped off buildings. Many more trees and branches will fall, and outages of power and other utilities will be significant.

Even a relatively mild hurricane can cause significant damage to a community.

HURRICANES

A category four storm has wind speeds of 130 to 156 miles per hour (209 to 251 kmh). It is also considered a major storm. This type of hurricane will destroy roofs and collapse the walls of buildings. So many trees are knocked down that entire

neighborhoods may be isolated by blocked roads. Power and other utilities are likely to be out for extended periods of time.

The most dangerous storm is a category five. These hurricanes have wind speeds exceeding 157 miles per hour (253 kmh). They will destroy large numbers of homes, take down nearly all the trees in an area, and cause such severe damage that the affected area may be unfit for people to live in for several months. A storm's classification changes as its wind speed goes up or down. Sometimes hurricanes are downgraded to tropical storms by the time they reach land.

Prior to the 1900s, people had little or no warning about the approach of hurricanes or the potential damage they could cause. For example, in 1900 a devastating hurricane struck Galveston, Texas. Forecasters predicted the storm, but they could not predict the extreme storm surge that came with it. Six thousand people died. Today, oceanographers—scientists who study the ocean—and meteorologists use a number of

A category four storm, Hurricane Eta, struck Central America in 2020.

HURRICANES

Satellite photos show the Caribbean island of Barbuda before, *left*, and after, *right*, it was struck by the category five Hurricane Irma. Much of the island's vegetation and infrastructure was ripped away.

tools to track and predict hurricanes. These include satellite images, research ships, buoys floating in the ocean, radar, and aircraft that fly near and into storms. All of these resources gather information on temperature of the air and water, wind speeds, and the amount of water vapor in the air. With the help of computers, scientists can tell where a storm is, how large it is getting, and how it is expected to move. They can also predict where flooding and storm surges may occur.

The oceans are very large, and there can be a number of tropical storms in various stages of development at any time. To help make it easier to keep track of them, meteorologists give the storms names. In North America, an alphabetical list that alternates between male and female names is determined each year. The names of storms that cause very severe damage or loss of life are retired and not reused.

Hurricanes are extremely dangerous storms. When one is approaching land, government agencies issue warnings and

Crews that fly into hurricanes use sophisticated instruments to study the storm from within.

HURRICANES

instructions for evacuation. The best way to stay safe is to pay attention to these warnings and evacuate when instructed. It's important to note that sometimes even after a storm is downgraded below hurricane status, it can still cause damage. Storms that used to be hurricanes can still generate rain and cause flooding.

Places that get hurricanes often have infrastructure in place to prepare for evacuation when needed.

After Hurricane Katrina devastated New Orleans, Louisiana, in 2005, the storm's name was retired.

TORNADOES

Tornadoes are dangerous not just because of the winds themselves, but also because of the debris that the winds carry.

Tornadoes are dangerous severe weather events that come from thunderstorms. Some thunderstorms have very strong currents of warm air that rise to form the storm. They are called updrafts. These updrafts can sometimes cause the storm to rotate. When this happens, a rotating column of air forms. If this column reaches the ground, it creates a funnel of whirling winds, clouds, and debris that is known as a tornado.

Tornadoes can occur anywhere a thunderstorm can form. However, big thunderstorms called supercells are more likely to form tornadoes. Supercells form in areas where the air is warm and moist at the ground and cool and dry above.

Meteorologists watch supercells carefully for the formation of tornadoes.

TORNADOES

Like hurricanes, tornadoes are measured and categorized by their wind speeds. Scientists use the Enhanced Fujita (EF) scale to categorize tornadoes. This scale ranks tornadoes from EF0 to EF5. An EF0 tornado has wind speeds of 65 to 85 miles per hour (105 to 137 kmh). It can cause minor damage to roofs and trees. An EF1 tornado has wind speeds of 86 to 110 miles per hour (138 to 177 kmh). This type of tornado can result in slightly more severe roof and tree damage, and it can break windows. An EF2 tornado has wind speeds of 111 to 135 miles per hour (179 to 217 kmh). It is capable of tearing off roofs and taking down trees. An EF3 tornado has wind speeds of 136 to 165 miles per hour (219 to 266 kmh). It causes more extensive

Tornadoes can produce focused damage that destroys some buildings while leaving other structures nearby fully intact.

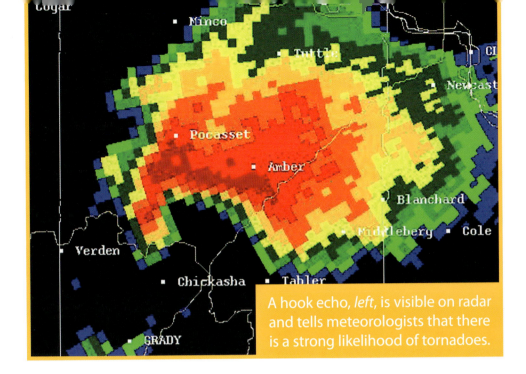

A hook echo, *left*, is visible on radar and tells meteorologists that there is a strong likelihood of tornadoes.

damage to houses and trees. An EF4 tornado has wind speeds of 166 to 200 miles per hour (267 to 322 kmh). These powerful tornadoes can level buildings and trees. The most powerful and deadliest tornadoes are categorized as EF5. Their winds spin at speeds in excess of 200 miles per hour (322 kmh). These tornadoes can cause catastrophic damage to structures.

Since tornadoes come from thunderstorms, the same methods for tracking those storms can be used to track and predict tornadoes. One especially good tool is radar. Meteorologists use radar to help map weather formations. The signal that bounces back when radar signals hit clouds and air masses is called an echo. Meteorologists watch thunderstorms for a hook echo, or a small hook shape at the end of the radar image of the storm cloud. It is usually found at the southwestern end of the thunderstorm. The hook shape is caused by the fast-spinning wind and rain that could become a tornado.

TORNADOES

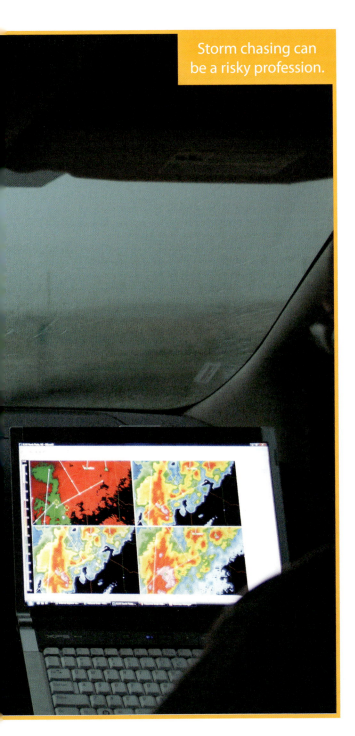

Storm chasing can be a risky profession.

Storm chasers have another important role in studying tornadoes. Professional storm chasers are scientists who follow active tornadoes. They take pictures and record observations that will help researchers learn more about tornadoes. This is especially important because the path of a tornado is hard to predict.

Tornadoes are very dangerous. They can develop fast and catch people off guard, especially people who are not monitoring weather reports. It is important to pay attention to tornado watches and warnings. People should seek shelter right away if a warning is issued. Those who live in areas where tornadoes happen a lot often have special shelters built in or near their homes. If no special shelter is available, experts say the best thing to do is to find a windowless room as far away from outside walls as possible. The lowest floor of a building is best. A basement, closet, or bathroom is often the safest choice. If people are caught outside, they should get out of vehicles. Cars and trucks can be blown by the strong winds. Experts recommend that people find a ditch or stay flat on the ground and cover their heads if possible.

Digging a storm shelter is one way people stay safe in tornado-prone areas.

Public places sometimes have designated tornado shelters.

HAILSTORMS

Hailstorms also come from thunderstorms. High up in the storm clouds, water vapor condenses to form ice crystals. Sometimes the wind is so strong that these crystals get bounced up and down high in the storm. Each time they go up and down, they pick up another layer of condensed water vapor and grow larger. If they become large and heavy enough to overcome the force of the wind, they fall to the ground as hail. If the hailstones are large, these storms can be dangerous.

Hail is often small in size.

Large pieces of hail can leave dents in cars that are parked outdoors.

Hailstorms usually last just a few minutes. Hail is usually about the size of a pea. However, it can be much bigger. Hailstones the size of golf balls can damage cars and buildings and destroy crops. When hail is more than 2 inches (5 cm) in diameter, the storm might also produce tornadoes. In extreme cases, hailstones can reach as large as 4 or 5 inches (10 or 13 cm). Hail this big can kill people and animals. Because hail is found in the same thunderstorms that produce tornadoes, scientists use the same methods for tracking them as they do for monitoring thunderstorms.

HAILSTORMS

Warnings issued for severe thunderstorms often include mentions of the potential for hail. Paying attention to these warnings is one of the best ways to be safe from hail. People often protect animals and cars by moving them to shelter. If people are outdoors when hail is falling, they should try to get indoors or under any kind of protection, such as a park pavilion or bus shelter. They should stay away from windows that could potentially be shattered by falling hail.

Hail can damage a home's siding.

A simple bus shelter offers protection against hail.

BLIZZARDS

Blizzards are the most severe events that occur in cold weather. Sometimes people call any storm with heavy snow a blizzard. However, there are specific things that need to be present before meteorologists call a storm a blizzard. Three criteria must be met for a true blizzard. First, the storm must have heavy snow. Second, it must also have winds in excess of 35 miles per hour (56 kmh). Finally, the storm must last at least three hours. Weather like this creates a dangerous situation in which the snow is so thick in the air that it is difficult to

Drivers in snowstorms experience reduced visibility.

see very far. True blizzards are very rare, even in many of the snowiest places on Earth.

Blizzards are very dangerous storms. The snow that comes with them can make driving difficult. So can blowing snow caused by high winds. The winds and heavy snow can also break tree branches.

In these ways, blizzards are similar to thunderstorms and other warm weather events. However, blizzards bring unique dangers not seen in warm weather. Getting caught outside

BLIZZARDS

Large accumulations of snow are able to collapse roofs.

in a blizzard can bring the risk of hypothermia and frostbite. Hypothermia is a medical condition in which the body's temperature drops below normal. It can be fatal. Frostbite happens when skin gets so cold it freezes. It can lead to the loss of fingers, toes, and other body parts with exposed skin.

Blizzards form when the ground and air are at freezing temperatures and a warm air mass moves over a cold air mass. Usually the cold air comes from the coldest areas on Earth near the poles. The movement of air at different temperatures creates a cloud. If this cloud has a lot of water vapor in it, snow forms. The movement of the warm air over very cold air creates wind. When enough wind and snow are created, a blizzard can form.

Meteorologists monitor blizzards in the same way they track other storms. They use satellites, radar, and equipment to measure temperature, humidity, and wind speed. Computer models are used to help predict how much snow a storm will produce. Trained observers measure and record snowfall in different areas.

Getting stranded in extreme cold weather is a life-threatening situation.

BLIZZARDS

Meteorologists watch winter storms for potential blizzard conditions and issue public warnings beginning 12 to 48 hours before they arrive. These warnings are rare and should be taken seriously. This extreme weather is dangerous in many ways.

Taking measurements in multiple areas gives meteorologists a better overall picture of a blizzard.

Even people inside buildings can be at risk during blizzards. Wind and heavy snow can damage roofs. They can also knock

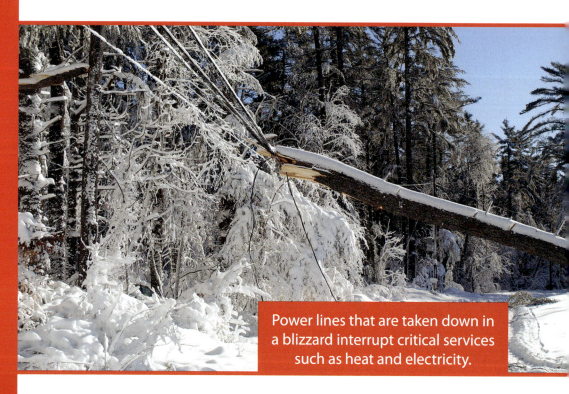

Power lines that are taken down in a blizzard interrupt critical services such as heat and electricity.

Keeping emergency supplies on hand is a smart idea when preparing for blizzards or other extreme storms.

down power lines. This can cut off heat and increase the danger of hypothermia. Downed power lines also affect the ability to use the internet, computers, and cable and satellite television. They can prevent people from charging their cell phones. A lack of power makes it harder to get information or call for help during a blizzard.

If the power goes out, people may use gas-powered generators or kerosene heaters to help keep their homes warm. These release carbon monoxide, an odorless, colorless gas that can be deadly if it builds up. Without proper ventilation, these devices can be dangerous.

Planning ahead for winter storms and blizzards can keep people safe. Flashlights, a battery-operated radio, and extra batteries, as well as warm clothing and blankets, help when the power and heat are out. These storms can last for several days. Even after the snow stops falling, it takes time for roads to be cleared. Having food that does not require cooking is

BLIZZARDS

important. Inspecting furnaces regularly, keeping generators outside and away from windows, and using a carbon monoxide detector can avoid the risk of carbon monoxide poisoning.

The greatest risk from blizzards comes from being outside. The cold, wind, and falling snow and ice create many hazards. Roads become very slick. Heavy wind-blown snow makes it hard to see. Eventually, the snow becomes so deep that vehicles get stuck. Shoveling and walking in heavy snow increases strain on the heart and can cause heart attacks.

People should take care to avoid overexertion when shoveling heavy snow.

Proper clothing helps people stay safe if they must go outside during a blizzard.

Preparedness is the key to staying safe outdoors during blizzard conditions. People should dress in layers if they must go outside. They should cover all exposed skin to protect against hypothermia and frostbite. They should stay off the roads if possible. If travel is necessary, experts recommend having blankets, extra clothes, food, and water in the car in case people get stuck. People at risk of heart attacks should not shovel or walk in deep snow.

ICE STORMS

Ice storms are extreme storms in which the main precipitation is freezing rain. They happen when the air close to the ground is below freezing. Snow falling from high in the atmosphere melts as it goes through warmer air above Earth's surface. The rain then freezes on contact with the ground. It coats every surface with slick ice.

All ice storms are dangerous. They often create black ice, a form of ice that is clear and hard to see on roads. Any ice

When roads become slick, the risk of accidents increases dramatically.

Ice that forms on power lines adds weight and puts intense strain on them.

on roadways makes them slippery and dangerous for driving. These storms can also have high winds. The combination of ice and wind can be very damaging to power lines and other structures.

Meteorologists determine how extreme an ice storm is by the thickness of the ice that accumulates. Severe ice storms leave ice more than 0.25 inches (0.64 cm) thick. The weight can knock down power lines and cell phone towers, pull

ICE STORMS

Trees are often damaged by heavy ice.

down wires, or make trees fall on wires and roadways. If a storm leaves 0.5 inches (1.3 cm) of ice, it can cause damage to trees and power lines that will take days to repair.

Ice storms are tracked like other storms. Meteorologists pay special attention to the temperature near the ground, since this determines whether the falling precipitation will turn to ice. They also monitor temperature predictions for the days following the storm. This determines how long it will take for the ice to melt.

Ice storm preparedness is similar to blizzard preparedness. People should stay inside whenever possible. If they must go outside, they should use extreme care driving or walking on icy surfaces. Being prepared for a power outage by having flashlights, radios, spare batteries, and extra food and water on hand is recommended. Ice storms can cut off power, and roads can stay dangerous for days. This is especially true if continued cold weather stops the ice from melting.

Putting down salt on walking surfaces after an ice storm helps melt the ice and prevent harmful falls.

DROUGHTS

During long droughts, the water levels in reservoirs become visibly depleted.

When an area does not have enough water because it has not rained or snowed there in a long time, it is called a drought. These conditions can be made worse by other factors, such as high demand for water from people or for livestock and agriculture. Sometimes the lack of precipitation lasts so long that the water levels in rivers, lakes, and underground water sources get very low. Droughts are different than most forms of extreme weather because they do not happen suddenly and they can last a long time. Sometimes it takes years for an area to reach drought status.

There are several possible causes for lower than usual levels of precipitation. Rain and snowfall depend on the right combination of temperature and moisture for storm clouds to form. Sometimes these conditions are affected by changes to other parts of the environment. For example, small changes in ocean temperatures can cause big changes in the amount of moisture in the air. Increases in the temperature of the ground affect the air currents and can cause water on the ground to evaporate. All of this helps develop a drought.

A prolonged lack of rain has a variety of causes.

DROUGHTS

Unlike many other extreme weather events, there is no set standard for a drought. This is because the normal amount of rainfall is different in different parts of the world. For instance, it could take years for a drought to develop in a desert that normally gets only a handful of inches of rain each year. It could take only a few days of reduced rainfall to start drought conditions on a tropical island.

Meteorologists use information about past and present rainfall to monitor the development of droughts. They also measure the amount of water present in rivers, streams, and

A drought in an arid desert looks much different than one in a lush rain forest.

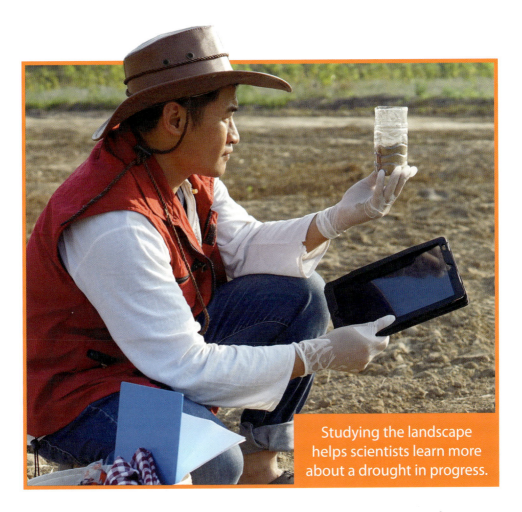

Studying the landscape helps scientists learn more about a drought in progress.

other bodies of water, including the water underground. Information about how much water the people, animals, and plant life in the area need is also studied. This helps predict how severe a drought is or might be.

Safety during a drought depends in part on where the drought is happening. A drought in a desert will be treated differently than one in a farming area. The most important step is usually finding ways to make up for the lack of available water. This is often done by government officials. They take steps such as releasing water from reservoirs or bringing in

DROUGHTS

During a severe drought in India in 2016, officials brought in water tankers to distribute water to residents.

water tankers. Droughts also bring special risks, such as the threat of wildfires caused by dry trees and plants.

Droughts are the second most destructive weather events in the United States after hurricanes. For example, a drought in 2012 destroyed more than $17 billion in crops and livestock. In countries that do not have as many alternatives for food, people often starve to death because of droughts.

Crop failure can be catastrophic to the people who rely on the crops for food.

155

WILDFIRES AND FIRESTORMS

Sometimes weather events cause wildfires directly. Other times, weather conditions make it easier for human-started fires to spread.

A wildfire is an unplanned fire that burns forests, grasslands, and other plant life. In some areas, they are called brush fires. People cause some wildfires by being careless with campfires, matches, or other sources of flame. Others are caused by lightning. They are more likely to happen during droughts. The dry conditions make it easier for trees and other plants to catch fire and burn.

Firestorms happen when a wildfire or brush fire gets so large that the flames create a hot wind. The air outside the fire is cooler and has more water vapor than the air in the fire. The heat of the fire draws this cooler, moister air into the fire. This movement creates wind, just as the movement of hot and cold air masses creates

Airplanes fly near wildfires to drop chemicals designed to stop the fires' spread.

WILDFIRES AND FIRESTORMS

wind in the atmosphere. The wind generated by a firestorm can create its own weather. A special kind of cloud called a pyro-cumulonimbus cloud often forms. The force of the wind also makes the air currents near the fire unpredictable. This can cause turbulence and is particularly dangerous to aircraft being used to observe or fight the fire.

Wildfires and firestorms are very destructive. They kill people, including firefighters, and animals. Large areas of forests and grasslands can burn. These extreme weather events also cause billions of dollars in property damage. They cause

Wildfires near populated areas endanger both residents and property.

disruption to utilities and transportation. They release smoke and ash that affects air quality for communities hundreds of miles away from the flames. This can cause breathing problems for people and even affect the weather. Wildfires are measured by the number of acres of land that are burned and the amount of property damage and loss of life they cause. Warnings are issued when a wildfire is threatening an area. The best way to be safe is to heed these warnings and evacuate if necessary.

Satellites in space keep an eye on the progress of a fire.

Meteorologists monitor the weather for droughts and lightning storms that can contribute to wildfires. A number of different agencies, including the National Park Service and firefighting organizations, keep watch on the ground. The National Aeronautics and Space Administration (NASA) also monitors the size and growth of wildfires using satellites orbiting Earth. NASA satellites gather information on how far the smoke and pollution from a fire spread and the extent of damage.

DUST STORMS

Dust storms happen when strong winds from a thunderstorm pick up dust from the ground. This can form a thick cloud of dust. Dust storms can happen anywhere thunderstorms happen, but they are most common in warm, dry areas. The American Southwest, the Middle East, and Australia are among the places where these storms typically occur.

An approaching dust storm can quickly cover a whole community.

In the 1930s, the United States experienced a severe drought. It turned the topsoil on millions of acres of ground in the nation's plains into dust, destroying vast areas of farmland. This caused what were known as black blizzards. These severe dust storms lifted the soil into huge clouds. The clouds traveled so far that ships in the Atlantic Ocean got a coating of dust from them.

Dust storms are measured by their size. Large ones can stretch thousands of feet into the air and cover miles of ground. When they are especially enormous, they are known as haboobs. This is the Arabic word for "blown."

Dust storms tend to happen very suddenly, and they can be difficult to predict in advance. Meteorologists monitor for wind conditions that could cause a dust storm and issue warnings when possible. Storms in progress can be tracked with radar and satellites.

In the 1930s, blowing dust got so deep that it buried farms in the Midwest.

DUST STORMS

A huge dust storm in Africa's Sahara Desert was visible from space in 1992.

These storms can be very dangerous. The dust can become so thick that it is hard to see and to breathe. Driving becomes almost impossible. The best way to be safe is to avoid moving into areas where dust can be seen in the air. These storms are often brief, lasting only a few minutes. If a person is caught out in a vehicle, experts recommend pulling off the roadway as quickly as possible. They also suggest turning off the car's lights to prevent others from thinking they can follow the lights through the storm and running into the parked car.

Trying to drive through a dust storm is very risky.

HEAT WAVES

During a heat wave, it's important for people exposed to high temperatures to keep hydrated.

Heat waves are two or more days in a row of extremely hot weather. The temperature that is considered excessively hot depends on the normal temperature in an area. It is often a temperature that people living in the area are not prepared for, meaning that it can be dangerous. People, animals, and crops can be harmed by the heat. Heat waves can be so intense that grapes turn into raisins before they are picked.

A heat wave happens when high-pressure systems hold warm air close to the ground. This keeps cooler air from moving in, so rain clouds do not form. The clear skies allow the sun to heat the ground even more, keeping the heat wave going.

Meteorologists use information about the past and present temperature of an area to determine whether a heat wave is happening. They need to know what the temperature usually is at that time of the year to decide if the current temperatures are higher than normal. After a heat wave is over, scientists gather information about its effects to determine how severe it was. For example, a 2003 heat wave in Europe was considered especially severe. After it was over, scientists determined that about 70,000 people had died from the effects of the prolonged heat.

A 2017 heat wave in Spain saw temperatures rise to 113 degrees Fahrenheit (45°C).

HEAT WAVES

Heat waves are tracked by monitoring the temperatures in an area. Meteorologists also watch the general weather conditions to see if the high-pressure system will move off and allow cooler air to come into the area. Heat waves can be more dangerous than people think. Some experts believe people do not take them seriously enough. Their concern is so great that

at least one country, Greece, considered naming heat waves, just as weather authorities name hurricanes. They hoped this would help people take them more seriously.

High temperatures cause people to lose water through sweat more quickly. This can change the balance of essential minerals in the body called electrolytes. This leads to nausea,

When a heat wave strikes, people look for ways to cool off.

HEAT WAVES

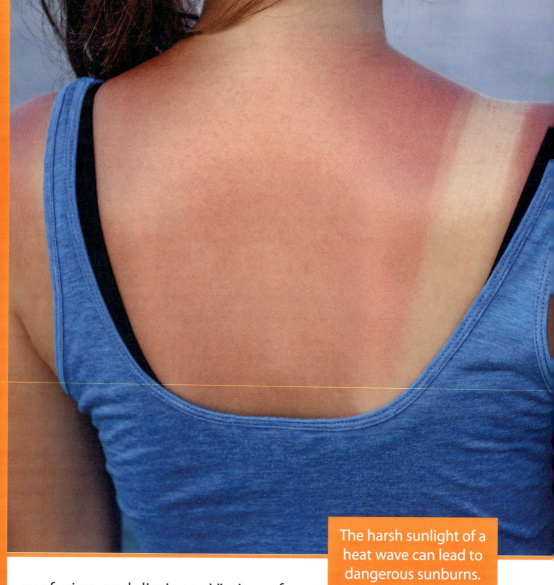

The harsh sunlight of a heat wave can lead to dangerous sunburns.

confusion, and dizziness. Victims of heat-related illnesses sometimes pass out. Older people, young children, and those with heart and breathing problems have particular difficulty dealing with high temperatures. The direct sunlight that comes with heat waves can also increase the risk of severe sunburns.

    The best way to stay safe during a heat wave is to stay indoors or in the shade. Drinking plenty of water is important.

Animals should also be protected from the sun and heat. It's especially important not to leave animals or kids in parked cars. The temperature inside can quickly become even higher than the temperature outside.

Animals and people alike seek shade during a heat wave.

SPECIAL STORM TYPES

There are other types of storms that fall into regular patterns. Meteorologists in certain areas see them so often that they give them nicknames. In North America, forecasters use nicknames like Nor'easters, Alberta Clippers, and others to talk about specific kinds of weather patterns. This makes it easier for people who are not meteorologists to understand the type of weather that is expected.

A Nor'easter can make driving conditions extremely dangerous.

Nor'easters can quickly erode beaches and damage buildings along the shore.

Nor'easters are storms that form very quickly with the help of warm, moist air from the Gulf Stream. The Gulf Stream is a strong ocean current that starts in the Gulf of Mexico. When warm air from the Gulf Stream reaches the Appalachian Mountains, it may meet cold air coming from New England. The result is a powerful storm with strong northeasterly winds that reach speeds greater than 50 miles per hour (80 kmh). Nor'easters can bring either heavy rain or snow.

SPECIAL STORM TYPES

Alberta Clippers start high in the mountains of the western Canadian province of Alberta. They move quickly across the American Plains and sometimes into the eastern part of the country. In the areas where they form, the jet stream does not allow strong low-pressure areas to form. These storms also tend to form in areas without much moisture in the air. As a result, Alberta Clippers are fast-moving storms that bring some snow, but not the heavy amounts often seen with Nor'easters.

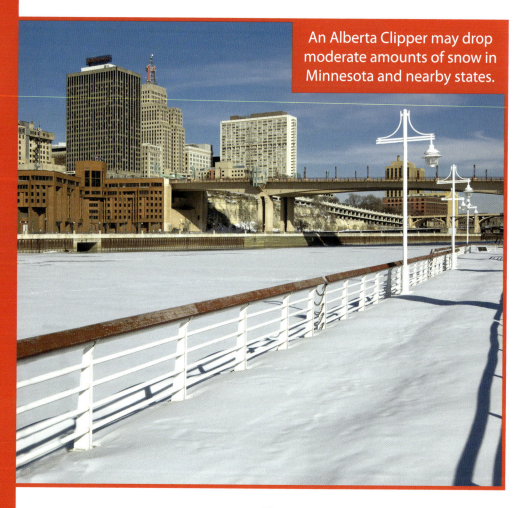

An Alberta Clipper may drop moderate amounts of snow in Minnesota and nearby states.

Panhandle Hooks can dump large amounts of snow in the Great Lakes region.

Panhandle Hooks are similar to Alberta Clippers. However, they form farther south in Oklahoma and the panhandle area of Texas. These storms pull in cold air all the way from Canada to west Texas. The cold air allows these storms to become stronger than Alberta Clippers. They are close enough to the Gulf Coast to pull moisture from that area. This means that Panhandle Hooks are usually the biggest snowmaking storms found in the Plains region. These storms often move across the country to the Great Lakes and beyond, allowing them to affect large areas of the United States. They get their name from their hook-shaped movement, starting by moving east and then hooking toward the northeast.

SPECIAL STORM TYPES

Explosive cyclogenesis occurs when the atmospheric pressure in a low-pressure area rapidly drops even farther. It is often called a bomb cyclone. This situation often happens when the seasons are changing. That's because those are the times of year with the biggest temperature differences

between warm air masses and cold air masses. The collision of these air masses makes powerful winds and pulls in a great deal of moisture. As a result, bomb cyclones often cause severe weather events, such as blizzards or strong storms.

Explosive cyclogenesis can lead to storms that disrupt transportation and daily life.

SPECIAL STORM TYPES

Intense snowfall from rare storms is disruptive to airline flights.

A 2019 bomb cyclone affected 25 US states. With heavy snow and wind gusts over 100 miles per hour (160 kmh), it knocked out power to hundreds of thousands of people and closed schools, businesses, and airports. It grounded 1,300 flights and caused widespread flooding. One meteorologist said it was like a 1,000-mile (1,600 km) -wide hurricane but with snow instead of rain.

Bomb cyclones are associated with heavy precipitation.

OTHER EXTREME WEATHER EVENTS

Not all extreme weather is a storm. Some atmospheric conditions just make storms more likely. They can also make storms stronger. El Niño and La Niña are climate patterns found in the Pacific Ocean. They can affect the weather almost anywhere in the world. These climate patterns happen in cycles and are not always present. They happen every two to seven years and can last up to a year.

El Niño results in warmer conditions off the coast of South America.

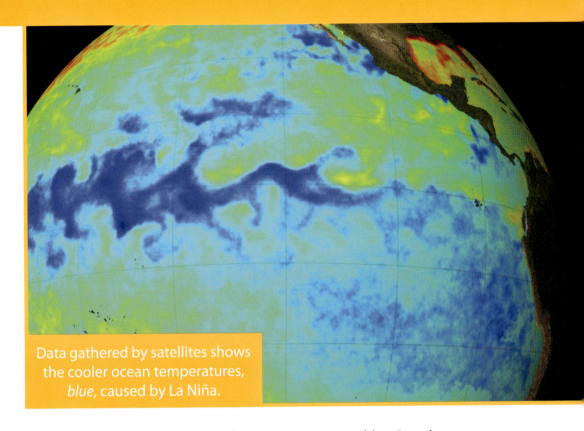

Data gathered by satellites shows the cooler ocean temperatures, *blue*, caused by La Niña.

El Niño happens more often. It was named by South American fishermen in the 1600s. They noticed that there were times when the Pacific Ocean's water was unusually warm. This often happened in late December. They named the phenomenon El Niño, a Spanish phrase used for the Christ Child, whom they celebrated at that time of year during the Christmas holiday. Later, an opposing pattern was observed. It was given the name La Niña, which means little girl in Spanish.

The warmer waters of the Pacific Ocean associated with El Niño make the jet stream move farther south. This causes more wet weather and flooding in the southeastern United States. It also causes warmer, drier weather in the northern part of the

OTHER EXTREME WEATHER EVENTS

United States and Canada. El Niño affects ocean life. The ocean warms up, so fish and plankton that need colder water stay away. Fish that prefer warmer water move into the area instead. Storms caused by El Niño in 2017 created a mudslide that wiped out an entire village in Peru. More than 800 Peruvian

El Niño can lead to erosion along the coastline, threatening cliffside homes.

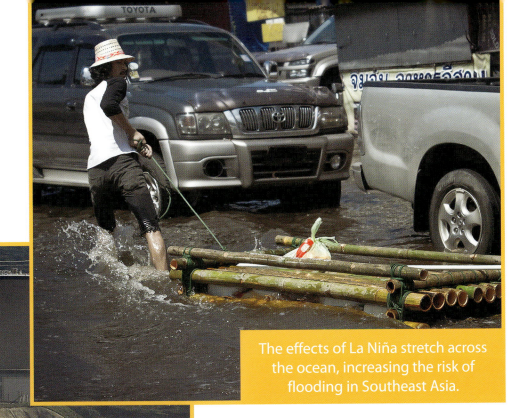

The effects of La Niña stretch across the ocean, increasing the risk of flooding in Southeast Asia.

villages were damaged and 85 people were killed in weather related to that El Niño cycle.

In La Niña, water temperatures push the jet stream toward the north. This causes weather patterns that bring heavier rains to Canada and the Pacific Northwest, while the southern United States sees drought conditions. The southern states also see milder winter weather, while the north sees colder winters. The colder Pacific Ocean water temperatures attract the cold weather fish again, while fish that prefer warmth leave for warmer areas.

OTHER EXTREME WEATHER EVENTS

Another extreme weather event is known as a polar vortex. This cold, low-pressure region of air circles the North and South Poles. Usually the vortex stays near the pole, where few people live to notice it. But sometimes it gets disrupted. It extends far enough that it affects areas with more people. When the air remains in these areas for a long period, it brings a period of extremely cold temperatures into areas that do not normally experience this. For example, in the winter of 2013–2014, a polar vortex that traveled farther south than usual kept parts of North America at below normal temperatures for more than three months.

A polar vortex can send temperatures plummeting to well below zero.

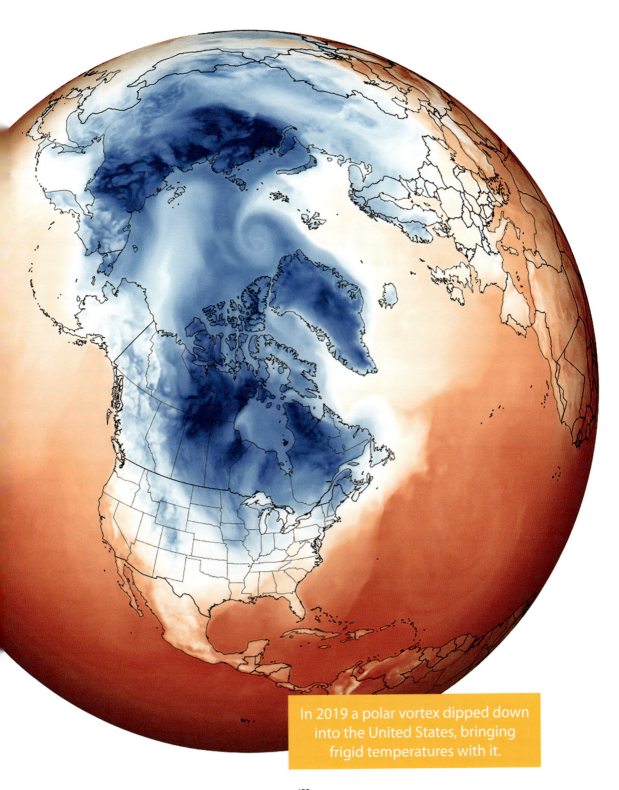

In 2019 a polar vortex dipped down into the United States, bringing frigid temperatures with it.

HOW CLIMATE CHANGE
IMPACTS EXTREME STORMS

Scientists did not keep records of daily temperatures until about 1880. Around that time, they also started recording information about storm activity. Scientists in the 1800s also began working backward to find out what the climate was like in ancient times. They used clues found in rock layers, the seafloor, tree rings, and fossils.

From this collection of evidence and some educated guesses about the climate in the past, today's scientists know that Earth's climate changes over time. In the last century they have observed a steeper-than-usual rise in Earth's average temperature. Scientists believe this is a result of human activity that accelerates the natural process of climate change.

Pollution from human activity has accelerated climate change.

HOW CLIMATE CHANGE IMPACTS EXTREME STORMS

Cars and factories release greenhouse gases into the atmosphere. These gases trap heat in the atmosphere by preventing the sun's energy from reflecting back into space. The result is global warming. Scientists say that even a few degrees of warming can make a dramatic difference in weather patterns because temperature is such an important part of how weather forms. In 2021, scientists determined that the previous seven years were the hottest years in recorded history.

Higher temperatures have been linked to extreme weather events. Scientists have seen clear signs that warming contributes to these events. They have noticed that heat waves

Climate change has resulted in conditions that make wildfires more common.

A warming climate makes hurricanes more frequent and more destructive.

have been occurring more frequently since the middle of the 1900s. Temperatures during these heat waves are warmer than in the past, and the waves often last longer. These waves of heat with little rain can mean increased droughts and wildfires. For example, in 2020 both the United States and Australia experienced wildfire seasons that were longer and more intense than normal.

Heat and moisture cause storms to develop, so scientists say that global warming can fuel more extreme storms. In 2020, 30 strong tropical storms started in the Atlantic Ocean. This was a record number for one year. Fourteen of them became hurricanes. Many experts think that global warming was an important factor in the number and intensity of these storms.

Global warming may also reduce the number of blizzards but increase other types of cold weather. For example, warmer-than-normal temperatures have been recorded in the Arctic. This can weaken the winds that keep the polar vortex contained to the area near the North Pole. In 2021, parts of Texas had record cold temperatures because the polar vortex dropped far south, bringing unusually cold weather with it.

GLOSSARY

air mass
A large body of air that moves together and maintains a certain temperature and humidity.

atmosphere
The layer of gas that surrounds a planet.

climate
The weather of a place over a long period of time, usually at least on the scale of decades.

convection
The process of heat transferring between hot and cold gases or liquids, which makes warmer air rise and cooler air sink.

diffusion
The process of particles of gas or liquid moving from an area where there are a lot of them to an area where there are fewer of them.

front
The boundary between air masses of different temperatures and densities.

global warming
The process of Earth's average temperature growing warmer over time.

greenhouse gases
Gases found in the air that trap heat from the sun; they include water vapor, carbon dioxide, methane, ozone, nitrous oxide, and chlorofluorocarbons.

high-pressure system
A region in the atmosphere with greater air pressure than surrounding areas.

low-pressure system
A region in the atmosphere with lower air pressure than surrounding areas.

meteorology
The science of studying and predicting the weather; scientists in this field are called meteorologists.

precipitation
Liquid or solid forms of water, such as rain or snow, that fall from clouds.

TO LEARN MORE

FURTHER READINGS

Drimmer, Stephanie Warren. *Ultimate Weatherpedia*. National Geographic Kids, 2019.

London, Martha. *The Effects of Climate Change*. Abdo, 2021.

Woodward, John. *Climate Change*. DK, 2021.

ONLINE RESOURCES

To learn more about weather, please visit **abdobooklinks.com** or scan this QR code. These links are routinely monitored and updated to provide the most current information available.

INDEX

air currents, 17–20, 35, 37, 55–56, 65, 67, 91, 104, 107, 126, 151, 158
air fronts, 18–20, 23, 48, 59, 91
air masses, 18–23, 40, 42, 48, 55, 60, 68, 91, 129, 140, 157, 175
air pressure, 11, 15–17, 57, 88–89, 116–117, 164, 166, 172, 174, 182
atmosphere, 10, 12, 14, 28, 30, 32, 34–36, 38, 43–45, 47, 50, 57, 68, 77–78, 80–81, 84, 86, 91, 117, 146, 158, 178, 186
aurora borealis, 84

blizzards, 4, 92–93, 95, 138–145, 148, 175, 187
bomb cyclones, 174–176

climate change, 24–27, 28–33, 34–39, 184–187
clouds, 41, 42–50, 52, 54–55, 57–59, 63, 64–65, 67, 68–70, 79, 80–82, 90–91, 107, 126, 129, 134, 140, 151, 158, 164
cyclones, 17, 117

dew, 64
droughts, 7, 9, 39, 150–154, 156, 159, 161, 181, 187
dust storms, 160–162

El Niño, 178–181

firestorms, 157–158
floods, 6, 39, 93, 94–95, 97–98, 106, 110–115, 116, 122–124, 176, 179
fog, 64–67
freezing rain, 58–62, 79, 146
frost, 64
frostbite, 140, 145

graupel, 58–59, 62
greenhouse gases, 34–36, 38, 186

hail, 58–59, 62–63, 105–106, 109, 134–136
heat waves, 164–169, 186–187
hemispheres, 13, 17, 84
humidity, 53, 55, 90, 141
hurricanes, 4, 7, 9, 91–92, 97, 99, 112, 114, 116–124, 128, 154, 167, 176, 187

ice storms, 146–149

jet streams, 20–23, 35, 37, 40, 172, 179, 181

La Niña, 178–179, 181

meteorologists, 15, 17–19, 22–23, 43–44, 86–93, 95, 107–108, 114, 118, 121–122, 129, 138, 141–142, 147–148, 152, 159, 161, 164, 166, 170, 176

Nor'easters, 170–172

oceans, 15, 26, 35, 66, 112, 117, 121–122, 151, 161, 171, 178–181, 187

power outages, 60, 106, 118–119, 121, 143, 147–148, 176

radar, 91, 98, 122, 129, 141, 161
rain, 5, 7, 24, 39, 41, 45–48, 52, 54–55, 57–63, 94, 106, 110–112, 114, 116, 124, 129, 151–152, 171, 176, 181, 187
rainbows, 68, 76–78, 81

safety, 71–72, 103, 108–109, 115, 124, 136, 143–145, 153–154, 159, 162, 168–169
satellites, 91, 98–99, 122, 141, 159, 161
sheltering, 7, 72, 109, 131–132, 136
sleet, 58–59, 61–62, 79
snow, 9, 24, 41, 47–48, 52, 56–58, 61–62, 94, 96, 112, 138–145, 146, 150–151, 171–173, 176
solar wind, 84
storm surges, 112, 121–122
sun dogs, 82
sun pillars, 82

tectonic plates, 29–30
thunderstorms, 48, 58, 72, 92–93, 104–109, 114, 117, 126–127, 129, 134–136, 139, 160
tornadoes, 4, 7, 9, 92–93, 97, 99, 105, 126–132, 135
typhoons, 117

volcanoes, 30, 33, 35, 72, 78

water vapor, 35, 42, 44–45, 48, 50, 52–53, 54–56, 64, 67, 68, 104, 107, 122, 134, 140, 157
weather forecasting, 86–93, 98, 100–101, 114, 121, 170
wildfires, 78, 154, 156–159, 187
winds, 7, 17–18, 20, 26, 50, 58, 89, 94, 105–106, 116, 118–122, 126, 128–129, 132, 134, 138–142, 144, 147, 157–158, 160–161, 171, 175–176, 187

PHOTO CREDITS

Cover Photos: Alex Prokopenko/Shutterstock, front (clouds); Vasin Lee/Shutterstock, front (lightning storm); Yegor Larin/Shutterstock, front (snowflakes); Minerva Studio/Shutterstock, front (tornado); Shutterstock, front (dust, hurricane, meteorology station, rainbow, weather background), back (windsock); Artur Synenko/Shutterstock, back (barometer)

Interior Photos: Shutterstock, 2, 3, 4, 7, 8–9, 11, 12, 13, 15, 27, 35, 37, 40–41, 42–43, 52, 53, 60, 61, 62, 63, 64, 70, 75, 83, 97, 98, 101, 107, 109, 111, 113, 119, 136–137, 140–141, 141, 142 (bottom), 146, 149, 153, 157, 164, 166–167, 168–169, 169, 172, 173, 176, 181, 186, 187; Kenneth Keifer/Shutterstock, 5; Vadim Lukin/Shutterstock, 6 (top); Noel V. Baebler/Shutterstock, 6 (bottom); Gritsalak Karalak/Shutterstock, 10; Aimur Kytt/Shutterstock, 14; Robert Adrian Hillman/Shutterstock, 16; NASA, 17, 23, 26, 30, 85, 91, 102, 116, 122 (left), 122 (right), 159, 162; Nick Julia/Shutterstock, 18–19; Menno van der Haven/Shutterstock, 20–21; Parinya Chaiwut/Shutterstock, 21; Claus Lunau/Science Source, 22, 25; Lukas Gojda/Shutterstock, 24; Johan Swanepoel/Shutterstock, 28; Mikkel Juul Jensen/Science Source, 28–29; Eva Kali/Shutterstock, 31; Vadim Sadovski/Shutterstock, 32–33; Marina Lohrbach/Shutterstock, 34; Rudmer Zwerver/Shutterstock, 36; Rich Carey/Shutterstock, 38–39; Marcus Wennrich/Shutterstock, 41; SSPL/Getty Images, 44; Aleksandr Simonov/Shutterstock, 45; Somyot Mali-ngam/Shutterstock, 46–47; John D. Sirlin/Shutterstock, 48–49; Stefano Garau/Shutterstock, 50–51; Shaun Wilkinson/Shutterstock, 51; Viktor Sergeevich/Shutterstock, 54; Andriy Blokhin/Shutterstock, 55; Bobkov Evgeniy/Shutterstock, 56; Lipatova Maryna/Shutterstock, 57; Jin Odin/Shutterstock, 58–59; Suzanne Tucker/Shutterstock, 59; Andrii Yalanskyi/Shutterstock, 65; Eddie Cloud/Shutterstock, 66–67; Ronald Verhage/Shutterstock, 68; QA International/Science Source, 69; Konstantin Grigorev/iStockphoto, 71; Ray Bond/Shutterstock, 72–73; Wesley West/Shutterstock, 74; Peter Maerky/Shutterstock, 76; Felix Nendzig/Shutterstock, 77; Roxana Bashyrova/Shutterstock, 78; Stuart Milliner/Shutterstock, 79; Mike Hollingshead/Science Source, 80; Kleymenov Valery/Shutterstock, 80–81; Juan Carlos Casado/Starry Earth/Science Source, 82; Bryan and Cherry Alexander/Science Source, 84; Leo Morgan/Shutterstock, 86; Sgt. Mike Meares/U.S. Air Force/Flickr, 87; iStockphoto, 88–89; Wattanasit Chunopas/Shutterstock, 89; British Crown Copyright/The Met Office/Science Source, 90; Michele Midnight/Shutterstock, 92; Alexey Stiop/Shutterstock, 93; Rouf Kuro/Shutterstock, 94–95; Roschetzky/Shutterstock, 96–97, 184–185; Jeff Greenberg/Universal Images Group/Getty Images, 99; NOAA/Science Source, 100, 129; Clarke Colin/Shutterstock, 102–103; Laura Hedien/Shutterstock, 104–105; Laura McCook/Shutterstock, 106; Anze Furlan/Shutterstock, 108; Dave Weaver/Shutterstock, 110; Erik K. Smith/Shutterstock, 112–113; Sean Hannon Acritely Photo/Shutterstock, 114; Steve Allen/Shutterstock, 115; NOAA/Flickr, 117; Nicolle R. Fuller/Science Source, 118; Jeiner Huete P./Shutterstock, 120–121; NOAA, 123; Darwin Brandis/Shutterstock, 124; Wesley Bocxe/Science Source, 124–125; Minerva Studio/Shutterstock, 126; Cammie Czuchnicki/Shutterstock, 127; US Air Force/NOAA/Flickr, 128; Beyond Images/iStockphoto, 130–131; Shae Cardenas/Shutterstock, 132; Lorenza Ochoa/Shutterstock, 133; Victoria Tucholka/Shutterstock, 134; Christian Delbert/Shutterstock, 135; Merrimon Crawford/Shutterstock, 136; Narongsak Nagadhana/Shutterstock, 138–139; Alexey Burakov/Shutterstock, 142 (top); Roger Brown/Shutterstock, 143; Wirestock/Shutterstock, 144; Joe Tabacca/Shutterstock, 145; Ted Pendergast/Shutterstock, 146–147; Irina Mos/Shutterstock, 148; Michael Vi/Shutterstock, 150; Minko Peev/Shutterstock, 151; Eloiza Fontes/Shutterstock, 152; Manoej Paateel/Shutterstock, 154–155; Inga Spence/Science Source, 155; Christian Roberts-Olsen/Shutterstock, 156–157; David A. Litman/Shutterstock, 158; Frank Zullo/Science Source, 160; Everett/Shutterstock, 161; Caleb Holder/Shutterstock, 162–163; Ruki Media/Shutterstock, 165; Shawn Hill/Shutterstock, 170; Rafael Macia/Science Source, 171; Lev Radin/Shutterstock, 174–175; Roman Mikhailiuk/Shutterstock, 177; Juan Gaertner/Science Source, 178; NASA Goddard/Science Source, 179; Jeff Chiu/AP Images, 180–181; Gary Whitton/Shutterstock, 182; NASA Earth Observatory/Science Source, 182–183

ABDOBOOKS.COM

Published by Abdo Publishing, a division of ABDO, PO Box 398166, Minneapolis, Minnesota 55439. Copyright © 2023 by Abdo Consulting Group, Inc. International copyrights reserved in all countries. No part of this book may be reproduced in any form without written permission from the publisher. Abdo Reference™ is a trademark and logo of Abdo Publishing.

Printed in the United States of America, North Mankato, Minnesota.
052022
092022

Editor: Arnold Ringstad
Series Designer: Colleen McLaren

LIBRARY OF CONGRESS CONTROL NUMBER: 2021952326

PUBLISHER'S CATALOGING-IN-PUBLICATION DATA
Names: Ungvarsky, Janine, author.
Title: The weather encyclopedia / by Janine Ungvarsky
Description: Minneapolis, Minnesota : Abdo Publishing, 2023 | Series: Science encyclopedias | Includes online resources and index.
Identifiers: ISBN 9781532198779 (lib. bdg.) | ISBN 9781098272425 (ebook)
Subjects: LCSH: Weather--Juvenile literature. | Meteorology--Juvenile literature. | Climate--Juvenile literature. | Encyclopedias and dictionaries--Juvenile literature.
Classification: DDC 551.5--dc23